QUESTIONED DOCUMENTS:
A LAWYER'S HANDBOOK

QUESTIONED DOCUMENTS:
A LAWYER'S HANDBOOK

Jay Levinson

ACADEMIC PRESS

A Harcourt Science and Technology Company

San Diego   San Francisco   New York   Boston
London   Sydney   Tokyo

ACADEMIC PRESS

A Harcourt Science and Technology Company
Harcourt Place, 32 Jamestown Road, London NW1 7BY, UK
http://www.academicpress.com

ACADEMIC PRESS

A Harcourt Science and Technology Company
525 B Street, Suite 1900, San Diego, California 92101-4495, USA
http://www.academicpress.com

ISBN 0-12-445490-9

A catalogue record for this book is available from the British Library

Typeset by Kenneth Burnley, Wirral, Cheshire
Printed in Great Britain by The Bath Press, Avon
01 02 03 04 05 06 BP 9 8 7 6 5 4 3 2 1

CONTENTS

This book is written in honor of

Dr David A. Crown,

dedicated mentor and loyal friend

FOREWORD

In the one hundred years of its existence, the profession of Questioned Documents examination has proven itself to be an important member of the forensic sciences. Today there is virtually no court of law in which testimony on document examination is not accepted.

This is not to say that every person claiming to be a document examiner is properly qualified to offer an expert opinion. As this book shows, the profession requires a number of skills. While the document examiner once concerned himself exclusively with handwriting, times have changed rapidly. Today the examiner must be familiar with computer printers, photocopy machines, facsimile printers, and all the other tools used to produce modern documents.

The classical books of Questioned Documents concentrate on handwriting problems and writing tools such as fountain pens which are little more than historical curiosity pieces in today's normal course of business. Reading classical texts is always important, but they must be taken in perspective, particularly in a dynamic profession such as this.

I am pleased to see that the *Questioned Documents: A Lawyer's Handbook* has surpassed traditional disciplines and addresses many of the practical issues that confront today's examiner. The volume is not designed to teach anyone to be a document examiner. Rather, it gives a concise picture of the profession today and a short index of basic literature.

May the reader use it well!

M. A. Kaplan (Brig. Gen., ret.)
Former Director of Crime Laboratories
Israel Police National Headquarters, Jerusalem

PREFACE

The purpose of this book is not to teach the field of Questioned Documents to people who are in search of a new profession. The focus is very specific – to explain to the lawyer some of the basics of document examination so that he or she is in a better position in court to present document evidence and interrogate his or her own and opposition witnesses. References are also made to professional literature, so that the lawyer can easily seek further information.

This volume is designed as a concise ready reference. When used properly it can give the lawyer a wealth of information very quickly, including some of the guidance needed to win cases in court.

Some of the material in this book covers technologies (such as the typewriter) no longer in common use today. It is the job of the document examiner to examine all documents, and not only those recently produced.

The bibliographies are by no means all-inclusive. They are meant as a first step to find further information on a particular topic.

ACKNOWLEDGEMENTS

The assistance of the Division of Identification and Forensic Science, Israel Police, is greatly appreciated. Dr Joseph Almog, Director of the Division, was kind enough to allow the use of illustrations, and staff members offered numerous constructive comments on the content of this book.

Russel Stockdale (England), David Ellen (England), Antonio Vega (Spain), Yaacov Yaniv (Israel), Jan A. de Koeijer (Netherlands) and Dr Bhandary (Nepal) were kind enough to render assistance, as were others who prefer to remain anonymous.

ABOUT THE AUTHOR

Dr Jay Levinson received his BA, MA and PhD degrees from New York University where he specialized in Near Eastern Studies.

From 1972 until 1981 he worked for the US Central Intelligence Agency where he was employed as a document examiner. During this time he became a member of the American Academy of Forensic Sciences and, after passing tests, a regular member of the American Society of Questioned Document Examiners. The American Board of Forensic Document Examiners also certified him as a diplomate. In 1981 Dr Levinson joined the Israel Police.

His basic training was with Dr David A. Crown formerly of Fairfax, Virginia (former president of the American Society of Questioned Document Examiners and of the American Academy of Forensic Sciences), and in an official training course at the FBI.

Dr Levinson has published more than 80 articles and papers dealing with document examination and forensic science. He has also given instruction in document examination in more than 20 countries and as an invited lecturer at several universities.

CHAPTER 1

INTRODUCTION

HISTORICAL SURVEY OF QUESTIONED DOCUMENTS

ENGLISH BEGINNINGS

Documents have been a part of western civilization since ancient times, and courts of law have considered documentary evidence for centuries. It is popular to cite ancient examples of authenticating documents, but this is nothing more than interesting trivia. Questioned Documents, as the profession is known today, developed during the nineteenth century.

In the realm of interesting facts frequently cited, a major legal step with strong implications for Questioned Documents examination was taken in 1562 when the English Parliament decreed forgery as a statutory offense. The damages incurred by forgery[1] were considered so severe that in 1634 it was made a capital offense[2], which it remained for more than two hundred years.

Thus, the crime of forgery was established in the sixteenth century, and in 1684 it was ruled that "comparison of hands is without doubt good evidence in cases of treason" (R v. Hayes, 10 State Tr 307). However, the expertise to examine cases was much later in coming. In 1762 the British court ruled, in effect, that handwriting is identifiable, and that a person in correspondence with someone can identify the handwriting of the correspondent (Gould v. Jones, 1 Wm Bl 384; 96 ER 216). The requirement of being "in correspondence" was nullified in 1911 (R v. O'Brien, 7 Cr App Rep 29, CCA).

One quirk in history is the question of who is considered appropriate to decide upon questions of handwriting identification. Initially that right was given to the jury (Solitu v. Yarrow, [1831] 1 Mood v. R 133, NP; Bromage v. Rice [1836], 7 C&P 548, NP). The idea continued. In 1864 a British court ruled that "an expert in handwriting should not be asked to say definitely that a particular writing is to be assigned to a particular person. His function is to point out similarities between two specimens of handwriting, or differences, and leave the court to draw its own conclusions" (Wakeford v. Lincoln [Bp] as reported in 90 LJPC 17C, PC). This idea lasted as long as 1918 when a Canadian court ruled, "It is competent for a judge and jury to compare the handwriting of a disputed document" (Rohoel v. Darwish, 1 WWR 627; 13 Altn LR 180).

[1] "Counterfeit" is based on Old French and acquired the meaning of non-authentic with recorded use in English as early as the fourteenth century. Today the term is used to describe non-authentic currency and other documents. "Forgery" comes from a Latin verb meaning "to manufacture," but by the fourteenth century it also had a meaning of making an imitation or a non-authentic product. The nominal form with this meaning, "forgery," is first found in texts from the sixteenth century. "Bogus," of unknown origin, is first found in the United States in 1827, when it is used to describe machinery used to coin non-authentic money. In this book the terms are used with the liberal interchangeability which they have acquired in modern English.

[2] Forgery was considered a threat to the Crown, since official Court documents were sometimes forged.

Simultaneously, however, a document examination profession began to develop. In 1863 an Irish court ruled, "The court refused to receive the [handwriting] evidence, and said that this case of evidence should be given by witnesses skilled in deciphering handwriting" (R v. Wilbain and Ryan, 9 Cox CC 448). Witnesses, though, were not totally trusted as a British court ruled in 1864, "The evidence of a professional witness is to be viewed with some degree of distrust, for it is generally with some bias" (Crosswell v. Jackson, 4 F&F 1, NP).

One of the earliest examiners was Charles Chabot, who in mid-century examined the Janius Letters (a case involving disguised writing reportedly dating back to 1769); it was this case and the carefully reasoned report of Chabot which would establish document examination in the English legal system.

THE PROFESSION DEVELOPS IN ENGLAND [3]

Modern Questioned Documents started out in England as the pursuit of private examiners. The first problematic case to reach notoriety for quite negative reasons was the Adolph Beck case[4], which caused major appeals and became a landmark in the development of English criminal appeals procedures. According to some sources the document examiner involved reached a conclusion based upon insufficient evidence. Quirke[5] and Mitchell also gained fame in their time, not so much for brilliant examinations as for the writing of books.

The Forensic Science Service, founded in 1935, was based upon already existing police laboratories in Bristol, Nottingham and Cardiff, where in the latter Harrison was chosen to head what was destined to be a major center for Questioned Documents. In the 1970s the central Questioned Documents Laboratory administration moved from Cardiff to Birmingham. (Most of the documents staff soon quit and established a private company – Document Evidence Ltd – which picked up a number of police contracts for Questioned Documents examinations.)

The Metropolitan Police (London) Laboratory was set up at roughly the same time, but a Questioned Documents capability began much later, in 1968. In 1995 the Metropolitan Police Forensic Science Laboratory (MPFSL) was subsumed by the newly created Forensic Science Service, which now has Questioned Documents Laboratories in Huntington, Wetherby, and London.

At some point a Laboratory of the Government Chemist (LGC) was also established to serve government offices such as the Post Office and the Department of Social Security; today its Questioned Documents Laboratory is located in Teddington.

Scotland had a different approach to Questioned Documents. There document examination (usually handwriting only) was done by uniformed

[3] This section is written with the assistance of David Ellen and Russell Stockdale (private correspondence).

[4] The fraud case evolved around a mistake between difference and disguise.

[5] Very much a graphologist who would not be accepted in modern Questioned Documents circles. See Quirke (1930), pp. 71–72 as an example.

policemen (fingerprint examiners) who worked outside the scientific forensic framework.

Parallel to the development of these government laboratories, a cadre of private document examiners also existed.

BIBLIOGRAPHY

Harrison, Wilson R. (1958), *Suspect Documents: Their Scientific Examination*, Sweet & Maxwell Ltd, London.

Mitchell, C. Ainsworth (1922), *Documents and Their Scientific Examination*, Griffin & Company, London.

Quirke, Arthur J. (1930), *Forged, Anonymous and Suspect Documents*, George Routledge & Sons, London.

QUESTIONED DOCUMENTS IN THE UNITED STATES

At the same time the examination of documents for court purposes was taking on the formalism of an independent profession in the United States. It was, in fact, in America that Questioned Documents established its strongest roots.

From all evidence available it was in the early half of the nineteenth century that courtroom testimony was first accepted on subjects which today are associated with Questioned Documents. American court records are sketchy; however the first descriptions of testimony seem to deal with the authenticity of handwriting and signatures. It was only in the 1870s that the courts even recorded the names of those people testifying.

A major factor which limited the introduction of Questioned Documents techniques into the courtroom was a rule derived from English common law, according to which comparisons could be made only between documents admitted into evidence for a purpose other than comparison. In simple terms, exemplars and specimens prepared to assist the examiner could not be entered into the courtroom. Slowly this rule was changed, and the profession of Questioned Documents began to develop.

Year	State	Case in which rule was changed
1814	Massachusetts	Homer v. Wallis (11 Mass. 309)
1831	Connecticut	Lyon v. Lymen (9 Conn. 55)
1849	Vermont	Adams v. Field (21 Vt. 256)

This process of legal decisions proceeded slowly, a major change occurring in 1880. The New York State Legislature formally changed the old rule by enacting a legal statute. Questioned Documents was given a "green light" to begin, and by the end of the century the names of expert witnesses such as Ames, Osborn and Hagan began to be heard frequently in the courtroom.

The importance of handwriting was supported in 1887 by Bell v. Brewster (10 N.E. 679, 44 Ohio St. 690) when the court ruled that a person can be identified by his handwriting. In the same year another court ruled (Gordon's Will, 26 A 268, 50 N.J. Eq. 397) that clear expert handwriting testimony is acceptable in court.

During the early period testimony slowly turned to other subjects in addition to handwriting. Toward the end of the century a precedent was set when ink examination was accepted for testimony, and in 1893 a New Jersey court made history when it allowed, in the case of Levy v. Rust (49 A. 1017), the first testimony on typewriter identification. By the 1890s Questioned Documents was a growing field, and the first books on the subject began to appear:

Hagan, William Elijah (1894), *A Treatise on Disputed Handwriting*, Albany, New York.

Frazer, Persifor (1894), *Manual for the Study of Documents*, Philadelphia.

Ames, Daniel T. (1899, 1900), *Ames on Forgery,* New York.

At about this time Albert S. Osborn, destined to be the dominant figure in Questioned Documents during the first half of the twentieth century, began to publish articles on Questioned Documents. In 1910 he published his classic work, *Questioned Documents* (better known by the 1929 revised edition).

1910	Osborn, Albert S.	*Questioned Documents*
1922	Osborn, Albert S.	*Problem of Proof*
1929	Osborn, Albert S.	*Questioned Documents* (rev.)
1937	Osborn, Albert S.	*Mind of the Juror*

Osborn began his career as an instructor of penmanship, eventually becoming a teacher of penmanship at the University of Rochester, but as early as 1887 he considered himself to be a questioned document examiner. From then until his death in 1946 he also published numerous articles on virtually every aspect of Questioned Documents and the presentation of expert testimony in the courtroom.

In 1913 Elbridge Stein, a penmanship teacher from Pittsburgh, wrote to

Osborn explaining that he was often asked about the authenticity of signatures. Osborn replied suggesting a meeting, which was held later that year. The circle of participants in the discussions soon widened. In recognition of Osborn's leadership in the field, in 1914 a larger group of document examiners began to gather each summer at his residence in Montclair, New Jersey to discuss professional matters and exchange experiences and ideas. As time passed it became accepted procedure that each year each participant would present a paper that was then discussed. On 2 September 1942 this group formalized itself as the American Society of Questioned Document Examiners, today the leading professional organization dealing with document examination and enjoying a broad international membership.

Two points should be stressed about this early period of Questioned Documents in the United States: (1) many of the examiners started as instructors of penmanship (Osborn, Stein, Walter), resulting in a very strong emphasis on handwriting in questioned document examination, and (2) all of the early examiners worked in the private sector. In fact, it was not until the 1930s that the first federal government laboratories were established, and 1938 when the City of Chicago opened the first major police Questioned Documents Laboratory. Lewis Waters of the Syracuse (New York) Police was the first non-private examiner elected to probationary member in ASQDE in 1948.

The most famous case of the period that really put Questioned Documents "on the map" in the legal profession was the trial of Bruno Richard Hauptmann for the kidnap/murder of the Lindbergh child on 1 March 1932 in Hopewell, New Jersey. In that case which opened on 5 January 1935 in Flemington, New Jersey, no fewer than eight questioned document examiners (Albert S. Osborn, Elbridge W. Stein, John F. Tyrrell, Herbert J. Walter, Harry E. Cassidy, Wilmer Souder, Albert D. Osborn, Clark Sellers) were consulted.

Today there is an extensive network of document examiners working in the United States. Many are employed by the numerous federal government and state/city police laboratories, which have grown up over the years after the early beginnings cited above. There are also numerous qualified examiners in private practice; these private examiners range from career private practitioners to retirees from government service.

Questioned Documents testimony is accepted in both civil and criminal litigation in the United States. Over the years, however, there has been a recurrent problem of defining who should be considered as a document examiner for purposes of court testimony as an expert witness. Since the mid-1970s the American Board of Forensic Document Examiners has made an effort to "certify" qualified American-resident examiners. The court, however, still has discretion, and it is not obligated to recognize this certification.

The documents profession has also spread to other countries to the extent that there is hardly a country with a developed legal system which does not have document examiners. Certification programs are also underway in many of these other countries, usually as part of a broader quality assurance program.

Mention should be made of the German tradition of document examination. In the English-speaking world a cardinal principle has been the ability of a document examiner to handle all types of problems, whether they be handwriting, typewriting, or alterations. Only in recent years has this partially broken down due to the wide range of new technologies involved in document production. The historic German tradition has always made a distinction between handwriting and technical (all other) examinations; these are considered two different areas of expertise.

There are a number of bibliographies covering published Questioned Documents literature, including articles and books. (For conference papers see ASQDE in the Supplement to this volume.)

BIBLIOGRAPHY

Costain, John E. (1977), "Questioned Documents and the Law: Handwriting Evidence in the Federal Court System," Paper presented at the American Academy of Forensic Sciences annual meeting, San Diego.

Harris, John J. (1982), "A Brief Glimpse of Forgery, the Law and Document Examination in England before 1900," Paper presented at the annual meeting of the American Society of Questioned Document Examiners, Boston.

Osborn, Paul A. (1964), "Excerpts and Comments on Testimony by Document Examiners in Re State of New Jersey v. Bruno Richard Hauptmann", Paper presented at the American Society of Questioned Document Examiners, Denver, Colorado.

Scott, Charles C. (1948), "Recent Questioned Document Law," *University of Kansas Law Review*, 16(2): 68–139.

Scott, Charles C. (1975), "How the New Federal Rules of Evidence Affect the Document Examiner," Paper presented at the annual meeting of the American Society of Questioned Document Examiners, Colorado Springs.

Scott, Charles C. (1981), "Landmark Cases on Document Law," Paper presented at the annual meeting of the American Society of Questioned Document Examiners, Houston. For review of other court cases, see ASQDE papers 1953, 1983. Reprinted posthumously as "Some Landmark Cases on Document Law," *International Journal of Forensic Document Examination*, 4(3) (1998): 206–213.

BIBLIOGRAPHY – CLASSICS AND EARLY TITLES

Blackburn, Douglas and Caddell, Waithman (1909), *The Detection of Forgery: A Practical Handbook*, London.

Brewster, F. (1932), *Contested Documents and Forgeries*, The Book Company, Calcutta, India.

Frazer, Persifor (1894), *A Manual of the Study of Documents*, J.B. Lippincott, Philadelphia (and reprints as Bibliotics or the Study of Documents).

Hardless, C.E. and Hardless, H.R. (1919), *Faults and Fallacies in Handwriting Identification and Expert Evidence in India*, Cunnar, India.

Hingston, William E. (1909), *Forgeries and False Entries*, Roxbury Publishing Company, Boston.

Jones, Lloyd L. (1938), *Valid or Forged? Quick Aid to Decision on Questioned Writing*, Funk & Wagnalls, New York–London.

Lavay, Jerome B. (1909), *Disputed Handwriting*, Harvard Book Company, Chicago.

Osborn, Albert S. (1929), *Questioned Documents* (2nd edition), Boyd Printing Company, Albany, New York.

Saudek, Robert (1928), *Experiments with Handwriting*, George Allen & Unwin Ltd, London.

Zinnel, George H. (1931), *Forgeries – Handwriting: Something for Nothing*, Bureau of Engraving, Minneapolis.

QUESTIONED DOCUMENTS IN ISRAEL

Israel enjoys a common law system in which accumulated legal decisions and enactments from the Ottoman, Mandate, and Israeli periods all have validity. Under Israeli rule in Judea and Samaria the Jordanian legal system is in force in those instances where legal proceedings are handled in civilian, not military, courts; Egyptian law was valid during the Israeli rule in Gaza. The Palestinian Authority has the right to enact laws and set court precedence in the area of its jurisdiction. Questioned Document testimony has been known in the country since the first years of the British Mandate period.

Matters relating to personal status (marriage, divorce, etc.) are handled by religious authorities. The Jewish rabbinical courts are also open to hear civil claims in which all parties agree to abide by the decision and not use the regular judicial system. Moslem religious authorities have a parallel court system. Although it is theoretically possible to have a Questioned Documents matter raised in the religious court system, those religious authorities consulted could not remember a known precedent in Israel of a forensic QD expert having given testimony; one case is known in Australia in which such testimony was sought by those party to a case.

The Israeli judicial system has both Magistrate's Courts and District Courts over which there is a Supreme Court which handles appeals. In addition, there are numerous cases involving Questioned Documents matters which are tried in the military court system.

Before the opinion of an expert witness can be accepted in Israeli courts, it is necessary to show certain facts: (a) that the witness does, indeed, possess the required knowledge, and (b) how it was acquired (practical experience, formal study, etc.). This is necessary since expert testimony is allowed only on those subjects requiring specialized knowledge that can be of assistance to the court. Handwriting, for example, has been ruled to be such a subject.

It is the court that has the power to decide if the credentials of experts are sufficient, and even more important what weight should be given to the testimony of the expert. This is particularly critical since the expert will be testifying on technical subjects beyond the court's experience.

In his testimony the witness must not only declare his findings; he must also explain to the judge how he reached his conclusions, making available to the court all of the materials which he examined. Thus, the judge is "brought into" the examination performed, understanding the expert's chain of thought, his reservations, and his degree of certainty.

Until 1954 examiners spent a major portion of their time in courtroom testimony, however a legal change in that year allowed expert opinion to be presented in writing, with the expert testifying in person only at the specific invitation of the prosecution or defense. In accordance, therefore, with legal requirements, expert opinions submitted to the courts are accompanied by a short description of the expert's qualifications and a signed statement of honesty. Thus, written opinions are considered sworn testimony. In the Israel Police forensic laboratories, personal appearance in court is required in roughly 6% of cases in which an expert opinion is written.

It should be stressed that the court is under no obligation to accept an expert's opinion, whether it is submitted in writing or orally, even if there is no opposition witness. In cases of conflicting expert testimony, the court can choose that testimony which it finds most convincing. In Supreme Court Case 86/58 Fromm v. Rosenfeld P/D 13 477-8, it was ruled that the Court can reach a handwriting comparison even without the assistance of an expert.

For obvious demographic reasons most courtroom testimony tends to be in Tel Aviv, Jerusalem and Haifa, though appearances in other cities do occur. Two landmark decisions in Israeli courts best summarize the legal status of handwriting examination:

In Criminal Appeals Case 352/71 (11.6.72, 7.5.72) the Israel Supreme Court ruled:

1 The profession of handwriting examination is a practical science, and one cannot doubt in principle the ability of an expert to determine forgery.

2 Nevertheless, the possibility of error always exists, whether it be by ordinary witnesses or by experts.

3 It is possible to identify someone by his handwriting, provided that the examiner is an expert who knows the known handwriting of the person identified.

In Criminal Appeals Case 46/77 (25.12.78, 31.1.79) Buchwald v. Barclay's Discount Bank P/D (1) 715, 719, the Israel Supreme Court decided that a court can decide upon the validity of a signature based upon the testimony of an expert. The final decision, however, is that of the court. Handwriting examination is not a secret code, and the subject can be explained to judges who can weigh the expert's testimony and determine what importance it should be given.

Handwriting as sole evidence has been ruled sufficient for conviction in both criminal and civil cases.

Police experts testify in criminal cases. Since the police have the only government Questioned Documents Laboratory in the country, this laboratory also serves other government agencies, including the army/military police. There have been instances where the police have handled private cases for a fee. Charges are generally waived for cases of "national" or "cultural interest."

As a practical matter, personnel from the Israel Police give most Questioned Documents expert testimony. In the period of the British Mandate there was a QD capability, and that tradition was continued right from the first days of the Israel Police. Even in the first two or three months after independence, when only three or four people worked in what was to become the crime laboratory division, one of them was an experienced Questioned Documents Examiner who had worked for the Mandate Police.

There are a number of private practitioners (including police retirees) who offer their services. Here, as always, the potential client is warned to examine credentials carefully before hiring an expert.

BIBLIOGRAPHY – ARABIC

Al-Sharif, Ahmad As-sayd (1972), *Lectures on Counterfeits and Forgeries* (in Arabic), Dar Al-Muarif, Cairo, Egypt.

Hilal, Mohammad Redwan (1996), *Forgery and Counterfeit* (in Arabic), Alem Al-Kutub, Cairo, Egypt.

Othman, Mohammad Salih (1986), *Document and Currency Forgery: Scientific Methods of Detection* (in Arabic), Arab Institute for Public Protection against Fraud, Rabat, Morocco.

BIBLIOGRAPHY – DUTCH

Bijl, L. J. (1990), *Zo goed als echt (Almost Real)*, Koninklijke Vermande BV, Lelystad, Netherlands.

BIBLIOGRAPHY – HEBREW

Hagag, Yitzchak (1988), *Document Examination and Handwriting Comparison: Forensic Graphology*[6] (in Hebrew), Tamar Publishing, Haifa, Israel.

BIBLIOGRAPHY – ROMANIAN

Ionscu, Lucian (1973), *Expertiza criminalistic a scrisului*, Editura Junimea, Ia i, Romania.

Sandu, Dumitru (1977), "Falsul in acte. Descoperire si combatere prin mijloace Dumitru criminalistice", Editura Dacia, Cluj-Napoca; reprinted Lumina Lex, Bucuresti, 1994.

BIBLIOGRAPHY – SPANISH

Crues, Carlos (1986), *Falsificación de documentos en general*, Astrea, Buenos Aires, Argentina.

Mendez Vaquero, Francisco (1994), *Documentoscopia: Estudios de la Policía Científica*, Dirección de la Policía, Madrid.

Ruenes Fernandez, Rafael (1938), *Orientación científica en la prueba de autenticidad de documentos*, Ordenas, La Habana, Cuba.

Ruenes Fernandez, Rafael (1951), *Exámen de documentos dubitados*, Litografía Isídro, La Habana, Cuba.

QUESTIONED DOCUMENTS AS A COURT-ORIENTED DISCIPLINE

There are many different types of experts who know something about aspects of documents. The paper manufacturer, for example, can have a very extensive knowledge about the chemistry of paper. The printer can have an equally broad knowledge about the printing process. The schoolroom teacher can be expert in penmanship[7].

The questioned documents examiner differs from these experts, not only in what he knows, but also in the purpose of his knowledge. The focus of the examiner is on presentation of findings in the courtroom. This is the goal of his training; this is the reason for his methods. Others might have impressive credentials in the specific area of expertise, but their knowledge was gained for other purposes. The examination methods which they use might not necessarily be the most appropriate (or even acceptable) in court.

[6] *In earlier Hebrew there was no distinction made between handwriting examination and graphology, hence the unusual title of this book. In current Hebrew usage the distinction between the two fields is made, and "forensic graphology" would be a self-contradictory term.*

[7] *Note People v. Stapleton (281 N.E. 2d 76, 4 Ill. App. 3d 477) in which the court ruled that the handwriting testimony of a bank signature expert was reversible error.*

TRAINING OF A QUESTIONED DOCUMENT EXAMINER

Not everyone can become a qualified document examiner. It is commonly required today that a person chosen to train as an examiner have at least a bachelor's degree and a background in science, criminalistics, or language and expression.

It is a generally accepted principle that the training of a document examiner takes at least three years of full-time apprenticeship under a qualified examiner. There is no university or trade school, which trains an examiner, so learning is "on-the-job" under proper supervision. There are, however, various specialty courses that are offered periodically. These have the value of covering or updating a defined topic; they should not be construed as a replacement for on-the-job training. (There is at least one American correspondence school reportedly with numerous students abroad, which offers courses for document examiners, however the real value of this "training" has been seriously challenged. Under no circumstance should it be considered a substitute for proper on-the-job apprenticeship.)

There are several written subject outlines that have been developed for training programs. Essentially a proper program must take into account both a strong theoretical grounding with lectures, site visits and appropriate reading, and extensive practical experience gained through laboratory cases. (Site visits should include paper manufacture, pen assembly, typewriter manufacture, printing methods, etc.; case experience should cover the widest range of Questioned Documents problems and courtroom-like defense of conclusions.)

When a trainee begins a Questioned Documents program he or she should be given a broad overview of the field, so that he can gain a general perspective. This should be done by presenting the student with a written program, theoretical lectures, then coordinated assigned reading. After this initial stage the trainee is ready to understudy with a qualified examiner, first watching how cases are handled, then working cases under supervision. Merely placing cases in front of a trainee and teaching him as he goes along might give practical experience, but it does not provide an orderly and complete understanding of the profession.

Periodically every trainee should be tested to determine the level of his or her skills and areas where more intensive training is required.

One area of training should not be overlooked – courtroom presentation. It should never be forgotten that the ultimate aim of a document examiner is to convince the court of his findings. "To convince" is not merely to read an expert opinion to the judge; it is to explain findings in a way that the judge is certain that the conclusion is correct. And that takes training and practice.

Another area of training not to be overlooked is professional literature. The trainee should have a good understanding of books, articles, and resources in the field. A key tool for this purpose is the Questioned Document Article Database (QDAD) assembled by James Larner and incorporating other earlier databases (e.g. Mannheimer Bibliographie für Schriftvergleichung und Urkundenuntersuchung [Peter Baier et al., 1987]; RCMP Questioned Document Bibliography).

There is no steadfast rule to determine when a trainee is ready to be certified as a qualified examiner. This is very much the subject decision of his/her mentor. In no case, however, should a period of less than three years' full-time training be accepted.

A word should be added about continued training. Questioned Documents is not a static field. Although the rules of handwriting examination have remained basically unchanged for decades, most other types of examinations adapt themselves to new materials in the market place, and examiners, too, must keep pace with these changes. For example, key/bar typewriters were the standard through the 1960s, and single element machines were the mainstay of the 1970s; the 1980s, however, saw the introduction of various types of printers into popular use; the 1990s were marked with computer-driven laser printers with fonts stored in the computer software. Examiners must keep up to date through reading, research, and participation in relevant conferences.

BIBLIOGRAPHY – TRAINING AND QUALIFICATIONS

Curvey, Clifford E., Epstein, Gideon, Quinn, Don O., and Moore, David S. (1976) "A Comprehensive Two-Year Training Program for Questioned Document Examiners," Paper presented at the ASQDE annual conference, Atlanta.

Gee, David (1988), "Training the Expert Witness," *Medicine, Science and the Law,* 28(2): 93–97.

Sellers, Clark (1966), "The Qualifications of an Examiner of Questioned Documents," Paper presented at the annual meeting of the American Society of Questioned Document Examiners, New York.

BIBLIOGRAPHY – BIBLIOGRAPHIC AIDS

Baier, Peter, Hussong, Jürgen, Hoffman, Elisabeth, and Klein, Michaela (1987), *Mannheim Bibliography of Questioned Document Examination,* Mannheim University, West Germany.

Herrick, Virgil E. (1960), *Handwriting and Related Factors: 1890–1960,* Handwriting Foundation, Washington, DC.

HIRING AN EXPERT WITNESS

Choosing the right document examiner to handle a case is not a matter of consulting the telephone directory and looking for the person with the most convenient address. If a legal matter is serious enough to warrant hiring an expert, it is certainly important enough to hire the *right* expert.

Many legal journals, both national and regional, advertise the services of document examiners. There are also specific forensic directories where examiners offer their services. These sources are usually no more reliable than the classified section of the telephone book. Listing is by paying the advertising fee, and not necessarily by meeting professional criteria. The best use of these resources is as an address book to send letters of inquiry asking for specific qualifications. QDEx, based upon work by Marvin Morgan, cuts short the process by listing memberships and employment history; this information should be verified and updated/completed before hiring an examiner.

One cannot look for an examiner with a university diploma in document examination, but one can look for an examiner with proper professional credentials. The lawyer should ascertain how the examiner was trained. Professional society memberships are an important tool to help keeping current with new developments in the field. Mere membership in a professional society, however, is not necessarily a measure of competence; membership by examination is much more important.

Certification by the American Board of Forensic Document Examiners (US)[8] and the Forensic Science Society (England) are gages of professional expertise. (ABFDE certification is restricted to North American residents; FSS certification has no residency requirement.) The American Society of Questioned Document Examiners stipulates regular membership on the basis of examination; a list of such members accepting private cases can be found on www.asqde.org. Efforts are being made to enable American judges to appoint experts for the court under the authority of Federal Rule of Evidence 706; these experts would be listed by the American Association for the Advancement of Science and the National Conference of Lawyers and Scientists, presumably in coordination with the ABFDE.

Not every examiner is qualified to handle every case. An examiner who is expert in handwriting might not be the right person to handle a case involving photocopiers.

It is not unreasonable for an examiner to investigate the background of a lawyer who wants to engage his services. It can be very problematic working for a lawyer with a reputation for dishonesty or unscrupulous behavior (not to mention problems in paying his witness).

The lawyer should ascertain that the examiner has access to an adequate

[8] *The procedures of the ABFDE are, themselves, under scrutiny. ABFDE works closely with the Forensic Accreditation Board (FAB) of the American Academy of Forensic Sciences. ABFDE is also looking into ways of having its operations validated by outside sources.*

professional library to answer questions, and to basic equipment (photography, microscope, etc.) as needed. Professional consultation with other examiners should not be neglected; very often discussing a case with another examiner can sharpen an opinion and raise questions, which might otherwise not have surfaced. Asking for a second opinion can at times be a safeguard against error.

A dignified appearance and effective courtroom presentation are also essential. If the examination was brilliant but the examiner cannot present his findings in a convincing way, there is a major problem. It is also important to find an examiner with properly balanced curriculum vitae; here, a list of publications, particularly in refereed journals, is a marked asset to show professional status.

It is not easy to find the right examiner, and when he is found the cost might well be more than expected. There are also no shortcuts to finding the right person. The best advice is for criminal lawyers to keep records of examiners with their qualifications, so when the need arises there is a data bank with which to start. Theoretically, all qualified examiners can render opinions on all questioned document issues. More practically, however, examiners often do develop areas of special interest and particular expertise (e.g. typewriters, photocopy machines, age of ink, etc.). This can be a significant factor in hiring for a case.

A word about fees. Private document examiners charge, and many exact considerable fees for their services. As one examiner phrased the matter, "The best costs!" Perhaps this is a bit crass, but the point is clear and needs no further amplification.

Is it ethical for an examiner to request a high fee? This has been a favorite subject at numerous meetings of document examiners, and the general consensus is that expertise costs money to obtain and maintain. Therefore, a qualified examiner should be appropriately remunerated (like the lawyers themselves!). There is one thing an examiner should never do – accept a case with payment dependent upon outcome of the trial or outcome of the examination. One side in the litigation might hire a document examiner; however, he is an objective expert. He should not be placed in the position of taking sides in the cases or even appearing to do so.

BIBLIOGRAPHY – EXPERT

Doud, Donald B. (1957), "Answering the Cross-Examiner on Expert Witness Fees," *Journal of Forensic Sciences*, 2(1): 88–93.

Harris, John J. (1988), "Some Observations on the Working Relationship between Document Examiners and the Attorneys Who Engage Their Services," Paper presented at the annual meeting of the American Society of Questioned Document Examiners, Denver.

Morgan, Marvin (1991), "Document Examiners," Paper presented at the semi-annual meeting of the Southwest Association of Forensic Document Examiners (SWAFDE), Phoenix, Arizona, October.

Scott, Charles C. (1982), "Amount of Fees Allowed Document Examiners," Paper presented at the annual meeting of the American Society of Questioned Document Examiners, Boston.

BIBLIOGRAPHY – LIBRARY

Tytell, Peter V. (1994), "Questioned Documents and Databases," Paper presented at the annual meeting of the American Society of Questioned Document Examiners, Long Beach, California.

WRITTEN DECLARATION OF EXPERT OPINION

When a document examiner issues a written declaration of expert opinion, that document has the same status of courtroom testimony. In many cases such a document is submitted to the Court in lieu of testimony, unless counsel requests such.

In addition to those statements required by law, the examiner should state clearly which documents were submitted for examination, and what were the conclusions. It is totally at the discretion of the examiner as to how detailed of a statement (if any) he wants to include regarding his reasons. For obvious reasons, private examiners tend to include longer statements; examiners in government or police service tend to be more concise.

From the lawyer's perspective, if there are no substantive questions to be asked on the written opinion, there is no reason to call the witness. It is pointless to call a witness merely for him to repeat his written testimony. (Expanding on that testimony to impress the court is quite another matter, since the lawyer has a very specific purpose in mind.) It should be remembered that there can very well be a legal penalty for summoning witnesses to testimony without substantive cause.

The written declaration is an important document in the trial, since it provides a clear statement of the examiner's opinion. (If, for some reason, the examiner changes his opinion, it is incumbent upon him to change his written statement as well.)

There are times when an examiner feels strongly about a point, but proof sufficient for an expert opinion is missing. In such a case the examiner can provide an investigative direction to the case; however this should be done not as a formal report of expert findings.

PREPARING FOR THE TESTIMONY OF AN EXAMINER

The use of a questioned document examiner can be an effective tool in a legal proceeding, whether the examiner testifies for the defense or for the prosecution. If the proper expert is chosen, he can be instrumental in convincing the court of particular facts about a document. The wrong examiner can be counter-productive in many senses.

It is not sufficient, however, merely to call the expert to the stand, swear him to honesty, and ask him to state his opinion. To maximize upon the effect of the testimony the summoning counsel should invite the expert for a pre-trial conference (and by "pre-trial" the intention is not five minutes in the courthouse corridor before the court session begins!). At that session the lawyer should review testimony with the witness and agree upon a basic set of questions through which the witness will slowly explain his findings. This is also the time to review any visual aids which the witness is going to present, so that they can be properly incorporated into the question and answer scenario.

From a practical point of view every session with the document examiner costs money. This, however, should not be a reason to neglect a pre-trial conference. If the witness is worth calling, it is also worth preparing the testimony. The worst thing is when an unprepared lawyer is surprised by the testimony of his own witness.

Lawyers should also realize that it is pointless to call an examiner for questions that need not really be asked. Likewise, examiners should be given the courtesy of advance notice when court dates are changed or when testimony is no longer needed due to agreement between the two sides in the case.

BIBLIOGRAPHY

Feder, Harold (1991), *Succeeding as an Expert Witness: Increasing your Impact and Income*, Van Nostrand Reinhold, New York.

Feder, Harold (1996), "Succeeding as an Expert Witness," *International Journal of Forensic Document Examiners*, 2(3): 214–219.

Hilton, Ordway (1957), "Effective Expert Testimony and Compensation for Expert Witness," *Journal of Forensic Sciences*, 2(1): 73–79.

Hilton, Ordway (1964), "The Essence of Good Testimony," Paper presented at the annual meeting of the American Society of Questioned Document Examiners, Denver, Colorado.

Lacy, George J. (1962), "Pretrial Conference between Expert and Attorney," *Journal of Forensic Sciences*, 7(4) (October): 507–515.

Osborn, Albert S. (1935), "Co-operation of Attorney and Expert Witness," *American Bar Association Journal* (March).

Sellers, Clark (1965), "Preparing to Testify," *Journal of Criminal Law, Criminology and Police Science*, 56(2): 235–240.

IN THE COURTROOM

Here the examining lawyer should once again remember the basic purpose of the testimony. It is not to recite; it is to convince.

In the role of witness the examiner must appear in a dignified manner that will lend credence to the testimony. His dress should be well chosen and neat. If the witness normally wears a police uniform, he may certainly wear it in court when he testifies on duty. Even though he is presenting unbiased expert opinion, he is still representing the police. He must speak in an unwavering voice and in clear sentences, always looking directly at the judge (or jury in countries where there is one). A witness who does not move his eyes off his notes makes a very poor impression. If the witness is inexperienced in these matters, he should be briefed in advance by the lawyer summoning him.

The first stage of testimony is to qualify the witness as an expert, and here no shortcuts should be taken. Although the basic expertise is described in the written expert opinion delivered to the court before the testimony, this is the opportunity to expand upon the witness's background, showing why the court should give strong weight to his testimony. If the opposition counsel is willing to stipulate to the witness's expertise, one should not stop this part of the testimony.

Next, the witness should explain exactly which exhibits he examined. This is a critical stage in making a clear and accurate presentation of work performed.

Finally, the lawyer and witness should develop the testimony through the question and answer exchange decided upon in the pre-trial conference. At all stages there should be an attempt to involve the judge in the examinations conducted by the expert. It is important that the judge understand the examinations conducted and how results were obtained. This will give the judge more confidence as he assigns weight to the expert's testimony.

If the testimony is properly conducted, the opposition counsel should have very little to ask in cross-examination. There should be an image of a document examiner whose professional qualifications cannot be assailed. There should also be a conclusion with a carefully prepared description of how it was determined.

Qualified opinions are certainly legitimate, since they are honest expressions of finding. The exact reasons for qualification should be cited. Most important, although the opinion might be qualified, it must be concise and to the point.

It should be noted that document examiners do not testify in court as often as one might think. Although private examiners do testify extensively, a survey has shown that only up to 6% (in most cases ± 2%) of cases in government/police laboratories lead to in-person court testimony.

BIBLIOGRAPHY

Eaton, David L. and Kalman, David (1998), "Scientists in the Courtroom: Basic Pointers for the Expert Scientific Witness," *Journal of Forensic Document Examiners*, 4(2): 100–104 (reprinted from *Environmental Health Perspectives*, 102 (1994): 668–672.

Osborn, Paul A. (1965), "The Trial of a Document Case," *Journal of Forensic Sciences*, 10(2) (October): 422–432.

Scott, Charles C. (1988), "Inconclusive Opinions as Viewed by the Court," Paper presented at the annual meeting of the American Society of Questioned Document Examiners, Denver, Colorado.

ILLUSTRATIONS

The question of whether illustrations should be used in testimony is best left to the expert witness in consultation with the summoning attorney. There is no basic requirement that an examiner bring illustrative material to the courtroom. The basic consideration is whether such material would assist the presiding judge(s) in understanding the testimony. The answer to that question is almost invariably positive.

One of the most commonly used illustrations is the enlarged photograph. This can be an effective tool, particularly when the document examiner can retrace his examination together with the judge. This should be done by the examiner on a large-size photograph which the judge should be able to see clearly from the bench; if smaller photographs are to be used, they should be supplied to the judge for further reference and for the court record, but not during the basic presentation.

Illustrations should also be properly mounted. After all, the document examiner is a professional, and he should present his testimony as a professional. Uncropped photographs stapled to a sheet and perforated for filing might be utilitarian in the laboratory, but they are very unprofessional in court.

At times an examiner might feel that basic teaching materials (examples of printing methods, diagrams of typewriter mechanisms, etc.) might be of assistance in rendering testimony. These materials can also be used in conjunction with testimony, but they should always be clearly sourced.

There are computer programs which can be used to help produce illustrative material. Documents can be scanned, sections enlarged, arrows or other indicated, etc. Overlays of signatures or typing/printing can be produced. These computer programs can produce very effective aids in court, but again it should be made clear to all concerned when computer-generated representations of evidence are being used. One word of caution: a computer-generated image retrieved by an optical scanner often lacks the fine resolution and detail of careful photography.

As mentioned, there is no absolute requirement that illustrative materials be used. If photo enlargements will not help clarify a point, they should not be used. If illustrations will only complicate testimony, they serve no purpose. After all, the role of the examiner as an expert witness is to explain the examination to the judge and convince him of the conclusion drawn. Whatever does not further the examiner in meeting this goal should be omitted from testimony.

In trials involving juries the same guidelines exist for the use of illustrations. If the witness decides to use some kind of visual aid, he should make sure that all jury members can see it clearly and understand what it is meant to show.

OPPOSING WITNESSES

Counsel should not be shaken if there is an opposing expert witness testifying for the other side in the case. Rather, certain calculated steps should be taken.

- Is the opposing witness a qualified expert? Numerous people have tried to testify in court without appropriate qualifications. In many cases they have actually succeeded. A careful check should be made of the opposing expert's qualifications to determine his true level of expertise. It is also proper to ask an opposing witness how he has supplemented his original training with new and updated information. This can be through reading professional literature and attending professional conferences.
- What did the opposing expert examine? One of the most common reasons for "differences" amongst experts is that there were differences in the materials examined. Sometimes one expert examines photocopies or only some of the documents examined by the other expert. Or, experts are given different "known" material upon which the examination is based.
- What is the precise opinion of the opposing expert? If the opposing expert is properly qualified and has examined the same documents, the differences in conclusions should be minimal. One examiner might express himself in slightly stronger or more qualified terms than another, but the basic conclusion should be obvious.

After counsel has asked himself these three questions, then he is in a position to determine his line of questioning in cross-examination.

Warning. If the opposing expert is to testify on a technical subject, it is critical that counsel have at least a rudimentary understanding of the subject so that proper questions can be asked.

BIBLIOGRAPHY

Conway, James V.P. (1964), "Voir Dire Examination of Document Experts, " Paper presented at the annual conference of the American Society of Questioned Document Examiners, Denver, Colorado.

Todd, Irby (1973), "Do Experts Frequently Disagree?" *Journal of Forensic Sciences*, 18: 455–459.

THE QUESTIONED DOCUMENTS LABORATORY

A private laboratory can be run very much according to the direction of its owner, obviously adhering to the principles of integrity and professionalism. A public laboratory, however, must be governed by the basic assumption that it is providing a service to other government offices (usually in the investigations and prosecution spheres).

Today, the "in" terms in management are "quality assurance" and "customer orientation," and there is no reason that a Questioned Documents Laboratory cannot adapt itself to these concepts. This is, in fact, for the general betterment of the laboratory.

Quality assurance

This is a concept related to total quality management and service. Not only must the examination be technically correct. It must be delivered properly to the customer and understood by him. Delays in delivering results should be explained so that the customer is satisfied with both the product and the accompanying service that he has received. Quality assurance is best effected by adherence to internationally agreed-upon guidelines and not the whims of laboratory directors. In forensic terms, the process begins with the search for evidence and covers such aspects as chain-of-custody and recording of the examination process.

Note: quality assurance means that the customer must be satisfied that he has received answers to the questions he has posed; it certainly does not dictate the *direction* of an examination decision.

Quality control

This is one aspect of quality assurance. There is a hard and fast rule in any professional situation – the work product (i.e. the QD examination) must be of the highest possible quality with absolutely no error. In some laboratories it is common that a second examiner review an opinion to minimize the possibility of error.

Customer orientation

The examiner should not be satisfied that he is giving the best technical report possible. He should place himself in the position of the requester and ask if he is giving the best service (pleasantness, courtesy, timeliness, clarity, etc.) possible.

Laboratory Accreditation

In various countries there are different means to determine that a laboratory is equipped and organized to give the service expected from it. This means that the laboratory must work according to approved procedures. An outside or independent authority such as another government agency gives this accreditation. In the United States crime laboratories are accredited by ASCLD (American Society of Crime Laboratory Directors); accreditation follows a procedure of pre-inspection preparation, inspection, re-visit, accreditation. In the United Kingdom accreditation is given by UKAS (United Kingdom Accreditation Services); in Australia NATA (National Association of Testing Authorities).

One requirement is that laboratory personnel undergo periodic proficiency testing, and not just a one-time examination similar to the entrance test for certain professional organizations. There are numerous types of proficiency tests: blind, re-examining, announced, etc.

One example of proficiency tests is the series run by the Collaborative Testing Service[9] of Herndon, Virginia; a problem with these tests is that some laboratories wish to guard their name (even when promised anonymity) rather than test proficiency, so the tests become group projects with effort devoted more than to a routine case.

The laboratory must also undergo periodic auditing to assure compliance with requirements. This insures that adopted rules are actually followed.

ISO

The International Standardization Organization (Geneva, Switzerland) has issued a series of directives standardizing laboratory and service products. ISO 9000 series details service and production standards. These are the guidelines which laboratories and forensic scientists are encouraged to follow.

ISO Guide 25, for example, provides guidelines for scientific laboratories. Again to cite examples, standards are recommended for calibration of analytical equipment, testing to establish known samples in examinations, etc.

It is certainly reasonable for counsel to interrogate a witness about laboratory

[9] *Began in 1975. Today CTS runs testing in collaboration with the ASCLD accreditation program.*

accreditation or certification, ISO requirements and recommendations, proficiency tests, and the auditing of the laboratory in which the examination in question was conducted. In theory, private laboratories can meet ISO standards and be accredited. In most situations this is not practical. Obviously, the private examiner essentially working alone without a large laboratory stands at a distinct *a priori* disadvantage.

Management trends follow waves of popularity. In any case a well-run laboratory will adhere to these basic principles, even if the "buzz words" do change periodically.

BIBLIOGRAPHY – QUALITY ASSURANCE

Clutterbuck, David and Kernaghan, S. (1991), *Making Customers Count*, Mercury Books (Gold Arrow Publications Ltd), London.

Levy, Shlomo, Levinson, Jay and Frank, Arie (1998), "Quality Assurance in a Monopolistic Environment: The Police Questioned Document Laboratory," *International Journal of Forensic Document Examiners*, 4(3): 202–203.

Stimpson, T.A. (1997), "Quality Assurance in Forensic Document Examination," *International Journal of Forensic Document Examination*, 3(3): 237–239.

CROSS-EXAMINATION

The question of cross-examination should be considered carefully by opposing counsel. Not all witnesses need to be cross-examined. If there is no clear line to the cross-examination, it is pointless to pound at a witness.

There are several areas where a Questioned Documents witness can be vulnerable:

- *Qualifications.* It is quite proper for counsel to attack the qualifications of an expert witness, however this should be done only when the attorney knows the witness' lack of qualifications. The need for exacting research is clear. Attacking a qualified witness is not only pointless; it can be very counter-productive.

  One point should be made about government experts. They must show that they are qualified in their own right. They should not be permitted to ride on the name and reputation of the laboratory which employs them. This is true both in terms of training and case examination, both of which can be challenged in cross-examination. On the other hand it is rare that a government laboratory will allow a totally unqualified person to testify. What does happen sometimes, however, is that someone testifies on a specific type of examination about which he has little experience. A tactic occasionally used by lawyers is to draw witnesses into areas beyond their expertise, then attack them when they are on uncertain ground.

- *Equipment.* Many private examiners might have had the appropriate training, but they lack appropriate technical tools to complete certain examinations.
- *Materials examined.* It is often the case that not every document in an office or a house is impounded as evidence. A selection is made, and that selection can have ramifications for the document examination. The documents an examiner has examined and the quality copy received can be critical points that are certainly valid to raise. Questions regarding chain of evidence can also be raised when this issue is relevant.
- *Conclusions.* If a lawyer attacks the conclusion of an expert witness, he should do so in close coordination with his own expert. This is a two-stage process – first to convince the court that the opposing expert has erred, then to call an expert and convince the court of a proper conclusion. An excellent way of determining what was examined and how is through a discovery motion.
- *Quality assurance.* In recent years there have been major developments to assure that courtroom testimony is competent and well presented. As already described, this means: (a) laboratory certification, (b) expert certification, (c) written work rules, (d) oversight. These rules were developed for larger laboratories, and now their application to independent experts is being studied. For example, it is not at all clear how a one-man private laboratory can be quality assurance certified. This entire area of quality assurance is a new and challenging area for cross-examination. (See Appendix I.)

The exact questions asked in each case should be structured as part of a basic argument, and there is definitely a function for an examiner to coach the lawyer with professional background and facts. Trick questions, however, should be avoided. After all, judges can spot trick questions, and they are seldom if ever impressed. What does impress is a well-presented line of reasoning in the questioning of a witness.

BIBLIOGRAPHY

Aron, Roberto (1990), *Impeachment of Witnesses: The Cross-examiner's Art*, Shepard's/McGraw-Hill, Colorado Springs, Colorado.

Black, David A. (1964), "Difficult and Troublesome Cross-Examination Questions," Paper presented at the annual meeting of the American Society of Questioned Document Examiners.

Imwinkelried, Edward J. (1982), *The Methods of Attacking Scientific Evidence*, Michie Company, Charlottesville, Virginia.

ETHICS

It is imperative that both laboratories and examiners conduct themselves in an ethical manner. An examiner should take care in his reports and testimony never to be influenced by financial interests or the desire of an investigator or attorney to reach a particular conclusion. Likewise, the examiner should never allow his expertise to be used to obfuscate justice. If another qualified examiner's conclusions are correct, it is an unethical misuse of knowledge to assist the cross-examination in discrediting the witness on the basis of "smart" questions.

No matter how extensive his background may be, no document examiner can know all the answers to all the questions. Thus, the examiner should respond clearly that he does not know an answer to a question when that is the case – whether it is to a client or to a judge. Needless to say, an examiner should never "make up" an answer; that is tantamount to perjury, and an expert witness who lies to the court even once, disgraces both himself and his profession. Even the hint of a lie or a special warning from the judge about perjury casts a strong and long-lasting negative shadow on the ethical conduct of the witness.

In short, a professional expert witness is an essential part of the legal system. As such, he must be beyond reproach. Even one instance of unethical behavior can taint an examiner for his entire career.

When an ethical question arises, the ASQDE Code of Ethics is a good document in which to find accepted guidelines.

BIBLIOGRAPHY

Hilton, Ordway (1988), "Document Examination and the ASQDE Code of Ethics," Paper presented at the annual meeting of the American Society of Questioned Document Examiners, Denver, Colorado.

Peterson, Joseph L. (1988), "Teaching Ethics in a Forensic Science Curriculum," *Journal of Forensic Sciences*, 33(4): 1081–1085.

RESEARCH

A truly professional questioned documents examiner will be involved in research. That is not to say that he will neglect casework or busy himself in abstract questions that have no practical application. The very opposite is true – research *is necessary* to handle cases properly. New questions arise. Not every point is already covered in existent literature. The purpose of research is to investigate new areas, to satisfy intellectual curiosity and ultimately increase knowledge in Questioned Documents.

One guideline in evaluating research is publication in peer-reviewed journals (given today's technology, either in "hard copy" or electronically disseminated). Peer-review is one measure of acceptance in the professional Questioned Documents community. Actually reading a person's publications can also be a valid indicator of his professional capability and competence, and his ability to express himself. Sometimes research is on a topic so specific that a journal will decline publication without prejudice to quality. For this reason some laboratories have a system of formal internal reports.

CHAPTER 2

HANDWRITING

INTRODUCTION TO HANDWRITING

Handwriting is a complicated operation that takes the average person many years to learn. Only over extended time can one develop the coordination of arm/hand/finger movements needed for what can be loosely coined the "handwriting of a literate person."[1]

When one "learns" a second script in a "matter of days," such as a European learning Arabic script in the first week of an Arabic course, the writer is essentially applying the motor and coordination skills learnt over the years to produce a new set of letters.[2] Writing characteristics learnt over a short period of time will also change rapidly as the writer acquires further skills. Since writing skills take so long to develop, they exert a strong influence on the writing of an individual. It is difficult to change movements abruptly to create different style letters. It is for this reason that the handwriting of a mature writer is *identifiable*.

Handwriting examination is not an absolute determination as one has in fingerprint or drug identification. In fingerprints a certain number of "points"[3] (the meeting of ridge-lines) in a continuous print constitutes an identification. In drug identification, particular chemical test results prove the identification of a substance. Handwriting identification, on the other hand, is subjective. Handwriting varies even in the same writer, and it is the subjective estimation of an expert based upon his experience that two writings were or were not made by one person (in technical terms, that the writing characteristics and range of variation are such that the writing could have been executed by only one person). There is no way to quantify the amount of experience necessary. Today that determination is generally made through proficiency testing and professional certification.

As a practical matter not all examiners have experience in all aspects of handwriting. For example, one examiner might not have seen many cases of simulated forgery. Another might not be acquainted with European handwriting systems applied to English. It is quite proper to highlight such problems in experience.

For many years handwriting examination constituted the major part of

[1] *The handwriting of a non-literate (semi-literate) person tends to be inconsistent, hence difficult to examine.*

[2] *Based upon this reasoning several examiners have deduced that writings in two different scripts (e.g., Hebrew/Arabic or Latin/Cyrillic) can be compared. It is true that movement will sometimes produce certain similarities, particularly of comparable letters, however other influences are such that the similarities should be viewed at best as class characteristics of writers knowing both scripts.*

[3] *The number varies according to jurisdiction and according to the purpose of the identification (e.g. connection with criminal activity, identification of a deceased person, etc.).*

questioned document laboratory casework. Although modern technology has introduced new types of examinations, there is every reason to believe that handwriting will continue to be a major segment of the caseload in many laboratories.

Some document examiners require only known and questioned handwriting to conduct an examination, while others are interested in learning details of the case. The latter approach allows the examiner to have a better gauge of factors (e.g. health, writing circumstances) affecting handwriting, as well as other possible questions regarding the document to be examined.

BIBLIOGRAPHY – HANDWRITING, GENERAL – ENGLISH

Huber, Roy A. (1982), "Handwriting Identification: Facts and Fundamentals (Parts 1 & 2)," Papers presented at the annual meeting of the American Society of Questioned Document Examiners, Boston, Massachusetts.

Huber, Roy A. and Headrick, A.M. (1999), *Handwriting Identification: Facts and Fundamentals*, CRC Press, Boca Raton, Florida.

Purtell, David J. (1982), "Glossary of Handwriting Terms," Paper presented at the annual meeting of the American Society of Questioned Document Examiners, Boston.

Rinsinger, D. Michael, Denbeaux, Mark P. and Saks, Michael J. (1989) "Exorcism of Ignorance as a Proxy for Rational Knowledge: The Lessons of Handwriting 'Expertise,'" *University of Pennsylvania Law Review*, 137: 731–792.

Rinsinger, D. Michael and Saks, Michael J. (1996), "Science and Nonscience in the Courts: Daubert[4] Meets Handwriting Expertise," *Iowa Law Review*, 21–74.

Smith, Edward J. (1984), *Principles of Forensic Handwriting Identification and Testimony*, Charles C. Thomas Publisher, Springfield, Illinois.

Wallner, T. (1961), "Experimentele Untersuchungen über die Reliabilität direktmetrisch messbarer Mandschriftenvariablen," *Zeitschrift für Menschenkunde*, 25: 49–78.

BIBLIOGRAPHY – HANDWRITING, GENERAL – ARABIC

Kamil, Ma'moun (1992), *Handwriting Forgery: Methods and Detection* (in Arabic).

Khalouf, Naif (1983), "Studies on Handwriting and Documents" (article in Arabic), Arab Institute for Public Protection against Fraud, Rabat, Morocco.

BIBLIOGRAPHY – HANDWRITING, GENERAL – SPANISH

Xandro, M. (1979), *Grafología Superior*, Ed. Herder, Madrid.

4 *This refers to US case Daubert v. Merrell Dow Pharmaceuticals, Inc., 509 US 579 (1993), which revised expert qualifications as stated in Frye v. United States, 293 F. 1013, 1014 (D.C. Cir. 1923). The qualifications for an expert were again dealt with in Kumho Tire Co., Ltd. v. Carmichael, 119 S. Ct. 1167 (1999). Also see US Federal Rule of Evidence 901(b)(2), permitting authentication by means of "non-expert opinion as to the genuineness of handwriting, based on familiarity not acquired for purposes of the litigation."*

FACTORS INFLUENCING HANDWRITING

The act of writing requires a complex series of skills and is also dependent upon various factors; as a result, it is a cardinal principle of forensic document examination that no two persons write exactly the same. (This is a basic supposition, which has never been fully proven statistically[5], yet entirely identical extended natural writing from two different persons has also not been found. A basic requirement associated with this principle is that the handwriting in question be sufficiently extensive.) Nor does one person ever write a distinctive signature or extended text exactly the same way.

According to traditional theory, handwriting can be broken down into *class characteristics* (features which are found in the writing of groups of people) and *individualities* (features particular to one writer). Class characteristics can range from features found in large groups of writers to those features that are found much less frequently. For example, letter formations based upon Spencerian penmanship can be considered a large group; trembling as a result of Parkinson's Disease is a much smaller group. Individualities include all deviations from school copy, such as changes in slant, loops, terminal strokes, etc. The writing of all people will have both class characteristics (e.g. letter formations based upon a specific learning system) and individualities.

It has been suggested that given the decline of penmanship as an art, the concept of "class characteristics" perhaps has a meaning different from previous years. If anything, this change in teaching decreases the amount of class characteristics to be found in a writing. Such characteristics, however, will always be found as long as handwriting is a taught skill. The increase in individualities certainly has ramifications for the document examiner.

It is the task of a document examiner to establish the writing characteristics (class and individual) and the range of a writer's variation (the "mapping" of individualities – for example, how wide is the lower loop of a lower case "f," or how low is a lower case "t" crossing slope).

To conceptualize *range of variation*, one can think of a bottle of ink spilling on a blotter. Most of the ink will be in one large stain, however there will be all types of spills in all directions. No matter how many times the ink spills, the same pattern will not reoccur. In handwriting, there will be all types of individualities but no two writers will ever produce the same range.

Differences are non-conforming aspects of writing in two documents that preclude the possibility that the two writings were prepared by the same person.

Sometimes there can be *idiosyncrasies* that are neither class characteristics nor individualities. For example, a break between two letters normally connected by the writer can be due to an external factor such as a telephone call or a knock on the door. Other continuing distractions, such as writing while talking on the

[5] *The issue of statistical studies of handwriting characteristics was raised in USA v. Roberta and Eileen Starzecpyzel (93 Cr. 553).*

telephone or watching a television program, can sometimes causes anomalies in writing due to lack of attention. Factors that determine how a person writes include the following.

TRAINING

There are numerous different handwriting systems that are being taught throughout the world. Although virtually all writers depart from the school copy system that they were originally taught, and they develop their own individualities, training still exerts a strong influence on writing.

Latin script

In the United States the common late-eighteenth and early-nineteenth century style was Old Round Hand, borrowed from England; in the nineteenth century the common penmanship style was Spencerian (developed by Platt Rogers Spencer [1800–1864] and based in part on Joseph Carstairs in 1814). In the early part of the twentieth century this gave way to the Austin Norman Palmer (1859–1927) method (first introduced in 1888), then to Zaner (died 1918)–Bloser (1865–1929) (first introduced in 1895 but popular only considerably later). There are also lesser known methods similar to Charles Paxton *Zaner*–Elmer Ward *Bloser*, such as MacLean and Strothers & Trusler. Thus, document examiners should have a solid knowledge of handwriting systems so that they can best determine the class characteristics of school copy.

At one time pedagogic thinking favored laborious penmanship lessons until as late as Grade 8, emphasizing motion and strokes to create a close imitation of the school copybook (which would be routinely disregarded from high school and onward as "mature writing" developed). Current thinking is to de-emphasize strict imitation of school copybooks, allowing for greater introduction of individualities in handwriting at an earlier age.

Since handwriting systems do change, school copy can be "dated," albeit only very roughly. In the modern era this is most notable with the almost absolute decline of the German *Frakturschrift* in favor of a more general European letter styling.

In recent years Palmer and Zaner–Bloser have also made inroads into Latin America where in many areas they have replaced the traditional Spanish hand as the system most often taught.

In England the most common handwriting system taught today is Modern Cursive, though it does have a number of similar variations. Modern Cursive is also the prevalent handwriting system taught in most Commonwealth countries with the blatant exception of Canada where systems closer to those in the United States are taught. Older British handwriting systems were Copperplate,

Civil Service (second half of the eighteenth century typified by Vere-Foster), Italic (Victorian Era popularized by Edward Johnstone) and Unjoined Scripts (beginning in the early twentieth century).

There are a number of other Latin script school copy systems (Germanic, French, Spanish) which are found throughout the world, although American systems are becoming increasingly more popular, and it is often possible to determine which tradition a student learned. (This is sometimes called "nationality of writer," though more accurately it is identification of the handwriting system(s) learnt[6].)

This determination, however, is particularly difficult when examining the handwriting of students in countries such as Israel, since frequently in the educational system students are taught English during their school careers by both American- and British-trained teachers. Due to the large number of immigrant teachers in English classes, it is often that a child is exposed to a variety of handwriting systems (including non-American/British), each with its subtle nuances, during the years that his Latin script is developing. The same phenomenon can be found in many parts of Latin America, Africa and the Far East.

[6] *Determination of nationality based upon linguistic characteristics such as word choice, syntax or grammar is outside the realm of Questioned Documents.*

BIBLIOGRAPHY – HANDWRITING SYSTEMS

Maclean, H.B. (1921), *The MacLean Method of Writing: Teachers' Complete Manual*, W.J. Gage & Company, Toronto.

Zaner, C.P. (1915), *Zaner Method Writing*, Zaner & Bloser Company, Columbus, Ohio.

BIBLIOGRAPHY – SCHOOL COPY SURVEYS[7]

[7] *A copybook exemplar collection in digitalized form is being prepared by ENFHEX.*

Piggott, Reginald (1958), *Handwriting: A National Survey (together with a plan for better modern handwriting)*, George Allen & Unwin Ltd., London.

Purtell, David J. (1980), "Modern Handwriting Instructions, Systems, and Techniques," *Journal of Police Science and Administration*, 8(1): 66–68.

United States Post Office (1953), *Foreign Handwriting Systems*, Bureau of the Chief Postal Inspector, Washington.

Cyrillic Script

This script, commonly associated with Russian but also found primarily in other Slavic languages, was developed by St Cyril of Salonika (826 or 827–869) (also known as Constantine the Philosopher) and his brother, St Methodius (825–885) in 863 under commission of Moldavian Emperor Michael III. The script was originally called Glagolitic, but following changes primarily by Clement of Ohrid, it became known as Cyrillic.

Hebrew Writing[8]

In Israel a typically modern version of Hebrew script is being taught in the country's schools. This is recognizably different from the Hebrew script of traditional Jewish communities abroad. Immigrants, however, often bring with them the Hebrew writing traditions of their country of origin. Traditional Eastern Hebrew script is quite distinct from typical European rabbinic hand, and the remnants of both can be found today, particularly amongst older writers.

An interesting factor in the Hebrew handwriting of many immigrants is that when Hebrew script is learnt at an adult age, many writers demonstrate characteristics usually associated with children. The reason is that they are "new" to the Hebrew script in which they have yet to develop skill.

In learning to write Hebrew script there is a definite tendency to stress form imitation and not arm movement (a key element in most English language penmanship). The net result is that although Hebrew is meant to be written from right to left, many immigrants in particular write the individual letters from left to right.

BIBLIOGRAPHY – HEBREW

Yaniv, Yaakov (1985), "Handwriting Class Characteristics of Arabs Writing Hebrew," Paper presented at IDENTA '85, Jerusalem, Israel.

Arabic Writing[9]

Arabic handwriting poses special considerations for an examiner. There are numerous styles of script. Although the average person writes in only one system, very skilled writers are sometimes able to write in more than one style. (There are no statistical studies examining the question of a very skilled writer transferring individualities between systems.)

Before handling an Arabic case, it is highly recommended that a document examiner have extensive knowledge of the Arabic script so that he can properly evaluate individualities and distinguish them from class characteristics.

Most commonly encountered Arabic script styles today are:

- nasx[10]. Modern standard printers type fonts are a version of this classical type style. Although the primary uses of nasx are in printing and typewriting, it is also used in handwritten documents. Many foreign or less schooled students of Arabic tend to imitate printed nasx in their handwriting.
- ruka'. This is a variation of tawki' script. Although probably Ottoman in origin, ruka' is the most common modern handwriting style in Arabic, particularly east of Libya.

■ shikaste. This is an extremely common Persian style, variations of which have also spread to Urdu and Pashto; shikaste has made only very minor inroads into Arabic language writing. The style of shikaste is so popular amongst Farsi speakers that in Arabic it is often merely called "Persian style writing."

There are numerous other handwriting systems in Arabic. They are primarily of historic interest or used only by calligraphers, or they are variations of Arabic script commonly associated with the writing of non-Semitic languages such as Malay. Turkish, once written in Arabic script, has been written in Latin script since the reforms of Kemal Atatürk (1881–1938) in the 1920s.

For the most part Arabic letters are connected, although there are several which are connected on the right but not on the left. Arabic penmanship prefers that the writer complete a word then return to its beginning to add marks such as dots (often two dots are written as a dash and three as a circumflex). Many people learning Arabic as a second language interrupt their writing to add the diacritical marks after each letter that requires them.

General

It is not possible to conduct an examination with a questioned text in one script (e.g. Latin) and known standards in another (e.g. Cyrillic), even though there might be letters common to the two scripts. Although certain characteristics are carried over from one script to another (typical features of Arabs writing Hebrew, Russians writing English, etc.), these are class characteristics which cannot form the basis of an identification. An examiner should resist the temptation of drawing conclusions from these letters in common.

Likewise, Latin block printing cannot be compared with Latin script. Hebrew "Rashi" script cannot be compared with regular Hebrew writing, although there are certain letters in common between the systems which might render possible suggestions.

BIBLIOGRAPHY – ARABIC

Levinson, Jay (1981), "Arabic Script," Paper presented at the annual meeting of the American Society of Questioned Document Examiners, Houston, Texas.

BIBLIOGRAPHY – EXAMINATION PROBLEMS

Crown, David A. and Shimaoka, Taro (1974), "The Examination of Ideographic Handwriting," *Journal of Police Science and Administration*, 2(3): 279–287.

Ellen, David (1972), *Handwriting Examination of Unfamiliar Scripts*, International Association of Forensic Sciences, Edinburgh.

Levinson, Jay (1983), "Questioned Document Examination in Foreign Scripts," *Forensic Science International*, 22(2–3): 249–252.

Tytell, Peter (1991), "Class Characteristics and Individualities: A Project Update," Paper presented at the annual meeting of the American Society of Questioned Document Examiners, Orlando, Florida.

NATURAL ABILITY

Not all writers have the same natural ability. Some writers have more dexterity in their fingers; others have less. Some writers have better shoulder-arm-hand-finger coordination; others have less. Thus, not every writer is capable of writing in "perfect" school copy. Smith lists the penmanship output of skill as controlling: size, slant, slope, spacing, shading, and speed. Other factors influenced by skill are the proportion of one type of stroke or letter to another, and alignment of the writing relative to the base line.

At one time, primarily in the first half of the twentieth century, it was in vogue to use measuring plates to record angles and slope. These plates are no longer in common use by mainstream examiners.

Skills fall within the general rubric of natural ability. Skills are learnt. No matter how well they are taught, they cannot exceed natural ability.

PHYSICAL CONDITION

Handwriting is also influenced by the physical condition of the writer. This condition can be temporary (such as intoxication or use of drugs), static (such as paralysis), or progressive (a continuing illness which becomes increasingly better or worse). Mental illness is also a factor which can definitely affect handwriting. During the second half of the twentieth century there were numerous studies on the effect of specific maladies (including drug use and intoxication) on handwriting.

Typical indicators of mental illness and intoxication are distortions in spacing, letter formations, and relative sizes of strokes. Physical illness tends to manifest itself in trembling, pen slippage (due to an inability to grasp the writing instrument), and changed letter formations (due to the physical inability to execute desired forms). These characteristics can emanate from a decrease in control over the writing instrument and/or a change in the perception of what is (or is to be) written. It requires a skilled and experienced document examiner to differentiate the normal writing of a seriously ill patient from intentional distortions.

There have been cases where a document examiner has been able to establish an approximate date of writing based upon the progressive deterioration of handwriting due to illness.

Extreme nervousness, heavy pressure (including the pressures of time), and strong tension can also influence handwriting. In all of these cases, however, a professional handwriting examination can usually yield enough individuality to form the basis of identification, on the condition that appropriate comparison materials also be available.

It should be remembered that document examination is a forensic science and not a medical science. A document examiner should not be called upon to give a medical or psychological diagnosis based upon handwriting traits. Related to this is the question of failing eyesight. This can be an explanation for "sloppy" writing with missed lines of intersection or wandering from the base line.

BIBLIOGRAPHY

Duke, Donald M. and Coldwell, B.B. (1965), "Blood Alcohol Levels and Handwriting," Paper presented at the annual meeting of the American Society of Questioned Document Examiners, Ottawa, Ontario.

Hilton, Ordway (1962), "Handwriting and the Mentally Ill," *Journal of Forensic Sciences*, 7(1) (January): 131–139.

Hilton, Ordway (1975), "Influence of Age and Illness on Handwriting Identification Problems," Paper presented at the annual meeting of the American Society of Questioned Document Examiners, Colorado Spings, Colorado.

Purtell, David A. (1965), "Effects of Drugs on Handwriting," *Journal of Forensic Sciences*, 10(3) (July): 335–346.

WRITING SITUATION

All writers do not react the same to all circumstances. Sometimes, the writing position (sitting, standing, leaning) has an influence on writing. A common example of this is signing credit card receipts in a supermarket, where the writer often has to lean over to a low surface and make room between his groceries, as he signs the transaction receipt. Another example is signing a credit slip seated behind the steering wheel of a car after filling the tank.

WRITING SURFACE

The writing surface can influence handwriting. For example, a rough writing surface can give the writing "tremors" in the line quality.

WRITING INSTRUMENT

This can also be an influence in writing. Some writers, for example, feel more comfortable with a thinner or thicker pen or pencil. Obviously, a faulty pen or a pencil with a very short stock can also influence the writing produced. A wider or thinner writing nib or point will also give a different appearance to the writing, sometimes with an influence over line or stroke shading.

BIBLIOGRAPHY – WRITING INSTRUMENTS

Girouard, Patricia L. (1988), "The Influence of Different or Unaccustomed Writing Instruments on the Act of Writing," *Journal of Forensic Document Examination*, 2(1–2): 13–22.

Mathyer, Jacques (1966) "Influence of the Writing Instrument on Handwriting and Signatures," Paper presented at the annual meeting of the American Society of Questioned Document Examiners, New York.

HABIT

Perhaps the strongest power in determining how a person writes is the force of habit. After he has learnt how to write, it is habit which strengthens skills. Accumulated habit can also move people away from school copy and into writing which is truly individual. This is closely linked to motor or movement skills.

LAYOUT

Habit also extends to how handwriting is placed on a piece of paper. This is manifest in the use of margins, relative placement of a signature following a text, etc. One place where this can be seen clearly is where handwriting commences relative to the printed text on a check. Obviously, even the strongest habit of layout can be changed when dealing with limited space available for writing.

CONCLUSION

Not all factors exert equal weight on handwriting, however when they are taken as a total package, the net results are as shown in the box on the facing page.

1   No person ever writes the same text exactly the same. Rather, the person writes with class characteristics and individualities that can be summarized into a certain range of variation in which there are consistent characteristics.

2   The range of variation of two people is never identical. Thus, it is the purpose of a forensic handwriting examination to determine a writer's range of variation and characteristics based upon known handwriting, then to determine if a questioned document is consistent with these findings.

CONDUCTING A HANDWRITING EXAMINATION

The examination of handwriting is just that – an examination. It is *not* a handwriting comparison. A professional examination is carried out as follows.

KNOWN HANDWRITING

If the question is being asked whether a specific writer wrote a particular text, the first step to be taken is to obtain the known writing of that person. It is best that this known writing be obtained from course-of-business writing (documents written during the normal "course of business" without any knowledge that they would be used as materials in a forensic examination).

Typical sources of course-of-business writing can be checkbooks, letters, appointment diaries, grocery lists, note pads, and personal telephone directories.

It is always desirable to have some course-of-business writing on hand for an examination, since this is the best guarantee that the specimen is normal writing. On the other hand, however, course-of-business specimens do have their limitations, and it may be necessary to supplement them with dictated texts to obtain certain words or letter combinations.

When no course-of-business specimens are available, it is legitimate to base an examination on dictated specimens. In such a case the examiner should be very keen to the possibilities of not natural or distorted handwriting.

Many examiners have their own systems of conducting specimen dictations. (In fact, there are examiners who do not wish to meet the writer at all so as not to be subconsciously influenced in the examination; these examiners will request that investigators obtain the specimens.) Some examiners prefer to ease someone into the writing process by asking him to write biographic material, while others prefer to begin with a standard text containing all letters of the alphabet. The classic version is the "London Letter," which was designed by Osborn for this purpose.

London Letter

Our London business is good, but Vienna and Berlin are quiet. Mr. D. Lloyd has gone to Switzerland, and I hope for good news. He will be there for a week at 1496 Zermatt St. and then goes to Turin and Rome and will join Col. Parry and arrive at Athens, Greece, Nov. 27th or Dec. 2nd. Letters there should be addressed: King James Blvd. 3580. We expect Charles E. Fuller Tuesday, Dr. L. McQuaid and Robt. Unger, Esq., left on the "X.Y." Express tonight.

Some examiners feel that the language in the "London Letter" is too artificial and stilted, posing difficulties for the writer and requiring excessive concentration on the text (particularly when dictated but permissible to present in printed or typewritten form), so over the years several variations have been developed. An example of an "improvement" is the "Idaho Letter" that was published by Osborn in the 1920s.

Idaho Letter

Dear Zach:

Well, the old class of "16" is through at last. You ask where the boys are to be. Val Brown goes on the 24th to Harvard for law. Don't forget to address him as "Esq." Ted Updike has taken a position with the N.Y. N.H. & H.R.R., 892 Ladd Ave., Fall River, Mass. And Jack McQuade with the D.L. & W. at Jersey City., N.J., 400 E. 6th St. Wm. Fellows just left for a department store position in Washington; his address is 735 South G Street. At last accounts Dr. Max King was to go to Johns Hopkins for a Ph.D. degree. Think of that! Elliot goes to Xenia, Ohio, to be a Y.M.C.A. secretary. I stay here for the present. What do you do next? How about Idaho?

Yours truly and Good-bye,

According to traditional thinking, after writing one of the above texts the writer is slowly introduced to the questioned text. (Today these and other similar texts are used extremely rarely.)

It is a cardinal principle that the person giving the handwriting specimen should absolutely not be shown the questioned writing before he completes his specimen writing. Even showing the writer a printed or typewritten version of a questioned text can influence such factors as spelling and capitalization.

Sometimes a writer will try to distort his penmanship in a specimen to avoid being identified as the author of the questioned text. The examiner should be aware of this possibility as the dictation is being conducted. The examiner should also insure that the specimen is not written in the awkward hand. These are examples of situations in which a document examiner can function much better than an untrained investigator.

From a lawyer's perspective, irregularities in obtaining handwriting can result in improper handwriting exclusions. They will generally not be the cause of an erroneous positive handwriting identification.

In all dictations several key rules should be followed:

1   The writer should be definitively identified (name, national identification card number or driver's license as applicable, etc.).

2   He should sign a statement that his writing is being provided by his own free will.

3   The writer should be given writing materials as similar as possible to those in the questioned document. If the questioned material is written, for example, in pencil on lined paper, those materials should be provided for writing the specimen.

4   The actual questioned document should not be shown to the writer to avoid the possibility of writing with intended distortions.

5   Whenever the writer is finished writing a segment, that material should be removed from his view. (When a writer is asked to sign a signature several times, it is best to always remove the page after writing. When this is not possible, one procedure is to ask him to use the paper from bottom to top. In this manner his arm covers previous writing.)

6   If the questioned document has been executed in cursive first let the writer execute his specimen as he sees fit. After one or two specimens one should instruct that further specimen writing be in cursive. If the questioned document is hand printed, so should the specimen. (This factor is not as relevant in Hebrew and particularly Arabic; although there is a "printed" form of Hebrew letters, it is not used as widely as Latin letter handprinting.)

It should be noted that an improperly conducted dictation session can void the validity of the specimens obtained and negatively influence examination results. For this reason it is essential to give investigators proper training when work considerations require that they conduct handwriting dictations.

Handwriting is a dynamic act that changes over the course of time. This change is most obvious, as noted above, when dealing with a progressively ill writer or younger people reaching the age of writing maturity, but changes occur in the handwriting of all of us. During the learning years handwriting changes constantly (though once someone is a "fluent writer" his handwriting can be examined). During the years of "writing maturity" change is slower, then it speeds up again during the "declining years." Specimens, therefore, should be prepared as close as possible to the date of the questioned material.

Although it is theoretically possible to identify a writing based upon specimens written at a time span of several decades, the longer the time interval is, the more difficult the examination is, and the more guarded the conclusions will be.

EXAMINATION OF KNOWN WRITING

Once the examiner has collected sufficient known specimens, the very first step is to examine the specimens to verify that the handwriting is normal writing. If the writing is judged not to be normal, the examination stops at this point. An assessment must be made, and new specimens must be obtained before the examination can proceed.

- *Normal writing.* If the examiner determines that the handwriting is normal, then he can proceed, obtaining a clear idea of the characteristics and variations. This is equally true for written text such as signatures.
- *Handwriting characteristics.* In conducting an examination the method used is to examine the letters and letter combinations, first determining the basic movement used by the writer (arcade, garland, angular, round, etc.). Then the examiner looks at the details of the writing.
- *Letter formation.* Where do specific letters start? How are they formed? Which letters are connected? – if any are, indeed, connected! Is the "samech" round or oval? What kind of an oval? Was it written clockwise or counter-clockwise?
- *Line quality.* Are the lines strong? Are there pen lift tracks? Does the writer appear to be "in control" of his writing? Do letters end smoothly or abruptly? Are curves awkward or free flowing? Is the writing fluent?
- *Pressure.* Is the pressure exaggerated? Is there more pressure on downstrokes (such as the terminal "nun") or on upstrokes?
- *Shading.* What kind of writing instrument has been used? Is there shading of the letters? Is the shading consistent? Which letters?
- *Slant.* Is the slant right to left or left to right? What is the angle? Is this common? Is there no slant at all? Are certain letters slanted more than other letters?
- *Proportions.* Are some letters much higher than others? Much lower? Is the vertical stick of the "aleph" much taller than the open circle? Is the final horizontal stroke of the initial/medial "nun" much longer than the vertical stroke?
- *Initial strokes.* Does the writer start with an extraneous initial movement "to get the writing going?"

- *Base line.* Where is the writing in relation to the base line? Is this consistent, or does the writing wander? Is this wandering random? Is there a general tendency to arch, curve, ascend, descend? Do certain letters tend to be higher or lower than the base line?
- *Frequent words.* Does the writer use certain abbreviations or pictographic techniques in writing familiar words such as "et" (accusative indicator) or "haya" ("he was")? NIS?
- *Special signs.* Is there a use of an apostrophe or vertical line to break the occurrence of "yod" followed by "hey" at the end of a word? "Aleph" followed by "lamed"?
- *Special marks.* How long is the comma? Is there anything unusual about the period? Is there anything noteworthy about other punctuation? Symbols (e.g. percentage or degrees)? How about the digits?
- *Speed.* Is the writing fluent? Are there pauses? Are these pauses always after the same letters?

The examiner should also pay attention to questions such as spacing between words, margins, etc., since these factors can also be typical of a writer.

Textual or syntax analysis has been used to identify writers. These approaches and their validity are outside the realm and training of the document examiner. They relate to the art of composition, rather than the physical act of writing that is the examiner's real expertise. Spelling errors are also in the realm of subjects outside the expertise of a document examiner although empirical experience shows that certain errors are nationality related (as the introduction of "y" in the Hebrew word for "shekel" by Arab speakers).

When the examiner is finished, he should have an accurate and complete conception of the handwriting of the known writer. He should know which class characteristics (features common to a large class of people) and individualities the writer uses. In short, he should have a clear concept of the writing and its range of variation.

Depending on the jurisdiction, many examiners keep working notes in their files. These notes are a memory jog and usually highlight the most salient points of an examination. In a proper examination the examiner takes into consideration so many facets of writing that it is impossible to record all of them in the case file.

EXAMINATION OF QUESTIONED WRITING

Now the examiner is ready to examine the questioned writing. Here, the first step is to determine whether the questioned document was all written by one writer and whether it also contains normal writing.

One writer

It is not a simple matter to determine the number of writers from a cursory examination. In essence, at this stage the examiner is not trying to jump to a conclusion. Rather, he is trying to define the basis of his examination. The example of a bogus check can be used. If there is an indication that the person who signed and entered the amount did not write the name of the payee (perhaps on the basis of different ink or gross characteristics of the writing), then the writing in the name of the payee should be excluded from the examination.

Normal writing

Just as in the case of the known writing, the examiner must determine if the questioned writing is normal. If the answer is that the writing is not normal, then the examiner must determine where there is:

- *distortion* – changes in the writing due to causes which might not necessarily be the fault or doing of the writer;
- *disguise* – a conscious effort to hide or change normal writing characteristics;
- *imitation* – the attempt to imitate the writing of another person.

If the questioned writing is not normal, the examiner can consider the possibility of asking for additional (more appropriate) specimens from the suspect. If, for example, the questioned writing was prepared by using the awkward hand (such as the left hand of people who normally write with their right hand), it might be beneficial to request that the suspect prepare a specimen accordingly.

As a general rule, many writing characteristics and habits found in writing with one hand are present in writing done with the other hand. This principle is true also with the very small minority of writers who can use both hands with equal comfort.

If the writing is normal, then the examiner uses the same procedure as in the known writing. He examines the letters and letter combinations, first determining the basic movement used by the writer. Then he looks at the details of the writing. He should know which class characteristics and individualities the writer of the questioned text uses. He should have a clear picture of the writer's range of variation.

When the examiner has completed this stage of his examination, then he is ready to answer the basic question, "Did the known writer prepare the questioned document?" If he has done his work properly, he should have a list of the individualities and range of variation of the known writing and a separate list for the questioned. He must then evaluate the two lists.

It should be mentioned that some examiners prefer to begin with the questioned, then look at the known. This is an equally valid approach, and it has various advantages, particularly in cases where there is questioned writing with several suspects.

BIBLIOGRAPHY – DISGUISE

Konstantindis, Siv (1987), "Disguised Handwriting," *Journal of the Forensic Science Society*, 27: 383–392.

Stevens, Viola (1970), "Characteristics of 200 Awkward-hand Signatures," *International Criminal Police Review*, 237: 130–137.

RESULTS

If there are unexplainable contradictions between the two lists, the suggested conclusion is that there are two different writers. If the two lists are complete and identical, it can be concluded that the person who wrote the known text also wrote the questioned text. If there are differences, this should be reflected in a less than certain conclusion.

The exact wording of a conclusion can be problematic, since the examiner must accurately convey his findings without any misunderstanding. In Israel an outline of eight degrees of certainty, from absolute identification to absolute non-identification, has been prepared by the police as an optional guideline to examiners. An explanation sheet is also available, describing the meaning of the terms used. (No system is absolute. The Birmingham [UK] Police uses a different set of degrees of certainty.)

An examiner is not required to reach a conclusion after every examination. It is perfectly professional to request further specimens or to find insufficient material for examination.

CASE NOTES

It is totally unprofessional for an examiner not to make notes as he conducts his examinations. Relying solely upon memory can invite mistakes. It is under-stood, however, that one cannot record every last finding.

Courtroom discovery motions can be a troublesome issue. The problem is that if a particular point is not recorded, the questioning attorney can try to show that perhaps the point was not examined or that the examination was incomplete. To avoid this potential problem, many examiners destroy their "personal" notes and leave in the case file photographs and only sufficient case notes to remind them how they arrived at a conclusion.

SPECIAL PROBLEMS

It is rare that a handwriting case does not have some unusual facet or special problem. These are just some of the considerations or types of questions which can arise.

SIGNATURES

The way someone signs his name can be quite individual. In simple signatures (where the name is simply written letter by letter) such as the letters which comprise the name, John Smith, there might be insufficient individualities to make a conclusive identification. In stylized signatures the examiner's job is much easier.

Many signatures are an illegible scribble, pictogram or design. It is not necessary to be able to read a signature (or a word for that matter) before examining it. The examination should concentrate on movement, relative positioning, type of stroke, etc., similar to a regular examination. If, however, a "signature" is inconsistent, this raises serious questions about an examination and the type of conclusion that can be reached.

Signatures Difficult to Read

Q.   Can you please read this questioned signature?

A.   No, this is not a legible writing. It is a design that Mr Doe uses as his signature. You can refer to K1-10 which are certified examples of Mr Doe's signature.

Q.   Can you show me the letters "oe" in his name?

A.   No, there these letters are not present.

Q.   Does that mean that you can examine writing that isn't there? Or writing that you can't understand?

The examination in a signature case closely parallels a regular handwriting case. Here, again, the importance of determining if the writing is natural should be stressed.

Initials should be treated just as a signature. If initialing is stylized and elaborate, there is more of a chance that an examination will yield a result than if the initials are written in a plain and indistinctive fashion.

Examining Initials

Q.   Could you please read the initials to the right of the third paragraph.
A.   Yes, they are "J.S."

Q.   And, in your opinion, who wrote those initials?
A.   I have specimen initials prepared by Mr John Smith. It is my opinion that he wrote the initials.

Q.   And you can tell that from such little writing? Just two letters and two dots?
A.   Yes, there are sufficient individualities to say that Mr Smith wrote the initials.

Q.   Really? You must be some expert to take two letters out of the alphabet and decide who wrote them!

Knowing a language and its orthographic rules can be important in examining signatures just as well as in examining extended text. In a case involving a will in Romania this point was very clear. According to Romanian Language Academy rules, the letter "â" was used as preferred spelling over its phonetic equivalent, "î" (except in "România") before 1954 and after 1990. In the case in question forgery was shown in part by proving that "î" had been transformed into "â" as part of the effort to show appropriateness of date.

Digits again pose a similar problem. Several isolated digits provide very little upon which an examination can be based. On the other hand, a ledger is generally enough for a handwriting examination.

BIBLIOGRAPHY

Harris, John J. (1957), "How Much Do People Write Alike: A Study of Signatures," *Journal of Criminal Law, Criminology and Police Science,* 48: 647–651.

Schwid, Bonnie L. (1994), *American Jurisprudence: Proof of Facts – Illegible Signatures and Writing in Litigation*, Lawyers Cooperative Publishing, Rochester, New York.

Figure 2.1

The full signature represents normal handwriting. In the enlargement note that the original "î" has been transformed into "â." This might conform with Academy rules, but not with the writing habits of the purported signatory to the will. (Courtesy of Mario Pop, Cluj, Romania)

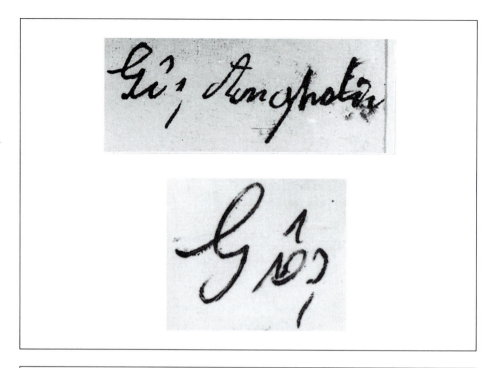

Figure 2.2

Some of the people in Nepal try to give trouble to other people for their vested interest and feel proud if they can make people appear in a court. A simple forgery with disticntly different signature and clearly unmatchable fingerprint (thumb impression is a usual practice in legal documents in Nepal). Photo (a): forged signature and fingerprint; (b): authentic signature and fingerprint collected in the presence of a judge in the court. A case of Mr Banti Lal vs Rampat.

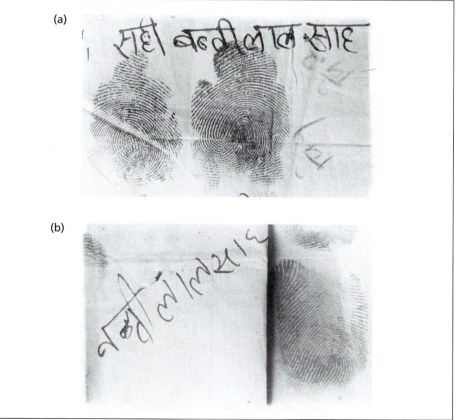

GUIDED HAND

It is recognized that in certain cases a literate person is unable to write due to physical condition, and another writer assists him or "guides" his hand. The inability has been described in three degrees of severity: inert hand, assisted hand, forced hand. Here there is no attempt at forgery. Rather, one person is simply assisting another with no ill intention. It is generally agreed that in these cases of guided hand there can be the writing characteristics of both the "writer" and the "guide"; as a matter of curiosity, research attempts have shown that the individualities of the "guide" are usually stronger than those of the "writer." In any event, however, these signatures are best authenticated by an eyewitness rather than by a document examiner.

BIBLIOGRAPHY

Foley, Bobby G. and Kelly, James H. (1975), "Guided Hand Signature Research," Paper presented at the annual meeting of the American Society of Questioned Document Examiners, Colorado Springs, Colorado.

Hecker, Manfred R. (1988), "The Taking of Handwriting Samples in Relation to Cases of Claimed Assistance in Writing," *Journal of Forensic Document Examination*, 2(1–2): 43–51.

Mathyer, Jacques (1975), "Handwriting and Signatures Made by 'Guided Hand'," Paper presented at the annual meeting of the American Society of Questioned Document Examiners, Colorado Springs, Colorado.

McNally, Joseph P. (1975), "The Guide is the Writer," Paper presented at the annual meeting of the American Society of Questioned Document Examiners, Colorado Springs, Colorado.

JUVENILE WRITING

Very often the question is raised as to whether the handwriting of a juvenile can be examined. The basic guideline is that once he has become a "fluent" writer, he will have developed his own consistent writing forms. Obviously, however, if he writes doggedly like school copy, there can be a situation where there will be no or insufficient individualities for an examination.

In using the term juvenile once should understand this as a euphemism for any person new to writing, or new to writing a particular script, regardless of his age.

COMPUTER-ASSISTED RECOGNITION

To date there have been several attempts to use computers in the recognition and examination of handwriting. These efforts tend to be in the experimental stage, often using bogus check files or anonymous letters as a database. The basic aim of these systems is to assist the examiner in locating handwriting samples for manual examination; there is no attempt to allow the computer to perform actual examinations. Three notable systems are those developed by the German Bundeskriminalamt (Wiesbaden) (FISH – conceptualization in 1977, development of model begun in 1982, operational application in 1990), SCRIPT (Netherlands) and the French National Police (Ecully).

There are several controlled access and check/credit card verification systems which operate based upon signatures. These systems are either static (based upon an existing signature) or dynamic (based upon controlled writing conditions such as computer-linked pen, pressure sensitive writing surface, etc.). They are not forensic systems. There have also been several attempts to source letters based upon the psycholinguistic characteristics of the author. Again, this effort has no connection to document examination.

BIBLIOGRAPHY

Hecker, Manfred R. (1986), "Forensic Information System for Handwriting (FISH)," Paper presented at the annual meeting of the American Society of Questioned Document Examiners, Savannah, Georgia.

Muenzenberger, M. (n.d.), "Forensic Information System Handwriting: An example for a classifying Search Process," unpublished paper.

FORGERY

There are several types of forged handwriting, which are typically found in questioned document cases. They can be categorized as follows.

MEMORY

There are instances when the forger has seen the genuine writing of a person, however the writing situation requires that he reproduce the handwriting from memory. In these instances either features of the forger's own handwriting or signs of distortion are generally present, perhaps with the exception of the most capable forgers.

SIMULATION

Here the forger views the known handwriting and tries to imitate it with his own free-hand simulation. Typical characteristics are slow writing with hesitations and stops-and-starts. While it is generally possible to determine forgery, it is usually difficult to identify the writer due to the heavy influence of copying.

The same usually can be said for school copy – when there is a determined effort to imitate the copybook, the individualities present are too few to allow for positive identification of the writer. (The question of school copy is purely theoretical, since classroom lesson books are by no means typical court evidence.)

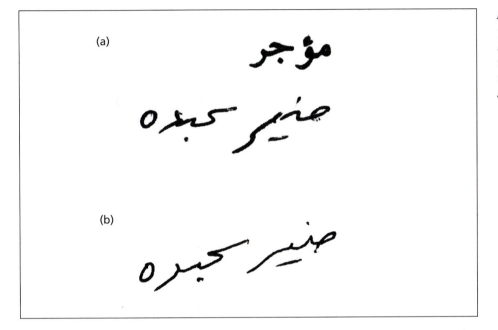

(a)

(b)

Figure 2.3
The lower signature (b) is a simulated forgery. The writing quality is slow and much less fluent than the genuine (a).

TRACING

Particularly with signatures the forger can place the genuine writing below his paper then trace over the writing. This also produces a hesitation and a writing that might be pictorially "correct" but produced with the wrong movement. Alternatively the forger can use a mechanical tracing device or place the genuine over his sheet of paper, write over the genuine producing indented lines on the sheet below, then fill in the indentations.

FREE STYLE

Sometimes, as can be the case with "found" checkbooks, the forger has no idea how the genuine writing looks. In this case the forgery will be simple free style writing, often with intended distortion to prevent identification.

In tracing it is very rare to be able to identify the writer, since the writing process generally disguises individualities. In free style forgery there is considerably more success.

Figure 2.4

Traced signature viewed with the aid of oblique light. (Courtesy of the Israel Police.)

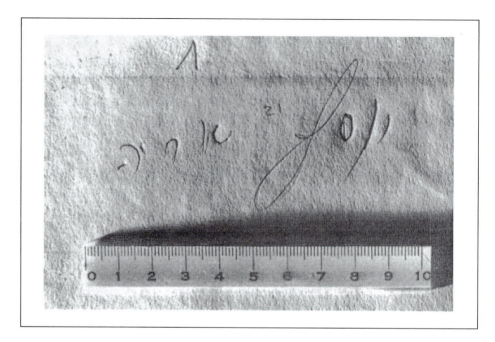

AUTO FORGERY

As strange as this might sound at first, there are people who have tried to "forge" their own signature. That is to say, they have written their signature in an unnatural fashion so as to deny the authenticity of the signature at a later date. This is a phenomenon found on check endorsements, contracts, bills of sale, etc. Typical features of this type of writing are back-slant or unusually narrow or wide loops. As a general statement, there usually are enough handwriting characteristics to associate the writer with the forgery.

Auto-Forgery

Q.   You state in your expert opinion that this is an auto-forgery.
A.   That is correct.

Q.   How many handwriting cases have you examined during your career?
A.   It is hard to give an exact number. I can say with certainty that I have examined at least five thousand cases.

Q.   How many cases involved auto-forgery?
A.   Five or six.

Q.   If a person examined five or six handwriting cases, would you say that he is qualified to examine handwriting?

A.   Of course not!

Q.   Then why are you competent to speak about auto-forgery with experience in only five or six cases?

WRITING LIFT

Today, in the age of the photocopy machine, it is possible to photocopy a signature, then "lift" the writing with cellophane tape before it is set. The signature is then placed on another document.

PHOTOGRAPHIC LIFT

There have been cases in which signatures, particularly of famous persons, have been reproduced on a forged document by photographic processes (e.g. photo-offset) or computer scanner.

SIGNATURE MACHINES

These machines are generally used to "sign" the name of a person to routine correspondence or form letters. For example, in a large company responses to customer inquiries might be machine "signed" by a senior company official. The unauthorized "signing" of a document is usually a criminal act of fraud. These signatures are generally recognizable by bluntness of strokes and absolute uniformity of the signatures produced.

BIBLIOGRAPHY

Cole, Alwyn (1973), "Auto-forgery," Paper presented at the annual meeting of the American Society of Questioned Document Examiners, Silver Spring, Maryland.

Conway, James V.P. (1982), "Authenticity vs. Simulation," Paper presented at the annual meeting of the American Society of Questioned Document Examiners, Boston, Massachusetts.

EFFECTS OF THE WRITING INSTRUMENT

At the beginning of the ball-point pen era some examiners thought that the use of such a pen would make casework more difficult. Today we have learnt that both the fountain and ball-point pens each have their own characteristics that can assist the questioned document examiner.

The typical quality of a fountain pen, whether ink loaded or cartridge, is the ability to shade as the nib changes direction. Under magnification the classic ball pen shows the roll of the ball, thus giving a clear indication of the direction of the writing. The laying down of lead from a pencil can also be used to show direction of writing, although this determination can be much more complicated.

In recent years porous tip pens have become common. At one point these pens only had broad tips and the popular name, "marking pens," described their basic use. Today, fine tips are available for general writing. The fine inking at the edges of a stroke as loose fibers touch the paper can identify these pens. (This does not happen with the metal nib of a fountain pen.)

A side benefit to the introduction of new materials to the market is the enhanced ability of a document examiner to set "earliest date" for the writing of a document.

BIBLIOGRAPHY

Snape, Keith W. (1980), "Determination of the Direction of Ball-Point Pen Motion from the Orientations of Burr Striations in Curved Pen Strokes," *Journal of Forensic Sciences*, 25(2) (April): 386–389.

INTERSECTING LINES

A frequently asked question is which of two intersecting lines was written first. To cite one typical example, was the signature written before or after the text with which it intersects? This question is also called "sequence of strokes" or "sequence of writing."

Numerous procedures ranging from lifting to high magnification have been suggested, however no real innovations have been made to answer this question. One research paper lists no fewer than thirty suggested methods. The basic guideline remains that unless there is clear evidence that one layer is on top of another (e.g. "clean" penciling atop an inked line), the eye, even when aided by strong magnification, will see what it wants.

From time to time examiners have written papers presenting new methods with good results (in tests conducted under essentially laboratory conditions). Before these methods are accepted in court, they should be viewed with scrutiny.

BIBLIOGRAPHY

Mathyer, Jacques (1980), "The Problem of Establishing the Sequence of Superimposed Lines," *International Criminal Police Review (Interpol)*, no. 342 (November): 238–250.

Poulin, Gilles (1992), "Establishing the Sequence of Strokes: The state of the art," Paper presented at the annual meeting of the American Society of Questioned Document Examiners, Ottawa, Ontario. Revised and published in *International Journal of Forensic Document Examiners*, 2(1) (1996): 16–32.

DO DOCUMENT EXAMINERS ERR?

For many years there has been a very justified professional examiners' tenet that a truly qualified person does not make a mistake in his casework. This is clearly a laudable goal, and every effort should be made to achieve it. Yet, history knows of errors even by the most qualified examiners.

The most serious error is to make an active decision that is incorrect. In other words, it is extremely serious to determine that someone did write something which, in fact, he did not. On the other hand, the inability to come to a conclusion when one is warranted is also an error, which can have serious consequences.

To avoid these situations it is imperative not only that an examiner work with patience. He must make a point of looking at the entire document and not only looking at one small point. He must avoid over-confidence, yet he must also have the self-confidence to make decisions whenever such are warranted.

This is certainly not to say that every examination should be routinely challenged in court. If there is reason to believe that there is a possibility of error, this should be addressed by a full examination conducted by another expert rather than a blind attack in court. A well-constructed and presented contrary opinion should be more convincing than merely casting doubt on the first opinion.

Experts will word their conclusions according to personal preference. As a result there might be variations in the perceived degree of certainty. This can be an avenue of court discussion in cases there the differences have true significance in the matter under discussion. The difference, for example, between "probably" and "quite probably" should be considered as stemming from the experience, training and judgment of an examiner. Choosing one rather than the other is certainly not a "mistake" meriting the testimony of a counter-witness.

BIBLIOGRAPHY

Kam, M., Wetstein, J. and Conn, R. (1994), "Proficiency of Professional Document Examiners in Writer Identification," *Journal of Forensic Sciences*, 39: 5–14.

Kam, M., Fielding, G. and Conn, R. (1997), "Writer Identification by Professional Document Examiners," *Journal of Forensic Sciences*, 42: 778–786.

Kam, M., Fielding, G. and Conn, R. (1999), "Effects of Monetary Incentives on Performance of Nonprofessionals in Document-examination Proficiency Tests," *Journal of Forensic Sciences*, 43: 1000–1004.

Osborn, Albert S. (1914), "Errors in the Examination of Handwriting," *American Law Review*, 48: 849–858.

CONCLUSIONS

When writing his conclusion, the examiner should carefully list those documents that he examined. This is particularly important since this forms the very basis of the examination. It has also been found that apparent disagreements between qualified experts often result from the examination of different materials.

Although a definitive conclusion is always the most desirable, it should be remembered that very often the examiner must qualify the results of his examination, as discussed above. There can be several reasons for this: limited writing available for examination, poor copies of documents, not natural writing, etc.

Sometimes what is needed is an interim opinion until such time as more material for examination is forthcoming. The problem with such an interim report is that it may well be much less conclusive than a final report, the latter being based upon additional material. In such a case it should be remembered that a qualified opinion on less material and a definitive opinion based upon more material do *not* contradict each other.

Even in a qualified opinion, however, the examiner should be very clear in wording his conclusion so that it is understood by all. Obviously, this forces the examiner to know exactly what he wants to say before he begins to formulate his opinion.

Some examiners, particularly in the private sector, write voluminous opinions. The length of a written opinion is not a reflection of the amount of real work invested in a case. There is, in fact, a school of thought that prefers shorter opinions restricted to legal requirements, a description of materials examined, and the "bottom line" of a conclusion.

A questioned document examiner is not a mathematician. Hence, he should not express his conclusions in terms of numeric probabilities, even if he uses words such as "probable" or "likely" in his opinions. Although this is done in DNA examinations, it is *not* accepted in Questioned Documents reports.

BIBLIOGRAPHY

Dick, Ron (1964), "Qualified Opinions in Handwriting Examination," Paper presented at the annual meeting of the American Society of Questioned Document Examiners, Denver, Colorado.

McAlexander, Thomas V. (1974), "The Meaning of Handwriting Opinions," paper delivered at the American Academy of Forensic Sciences, Dallas, Texas.

McAlexander, Thomas V. (1977), "Handwriting Opinion Terminology: A Layman's Guide," Paper presented at the annual meeting of the American Society of Questioned Document Examiners, San Francisco, California.

THE COURT

In the courtroom it is insufficient for an examiner to merely state his professional qualifications and examination conclusions. He must "involve" the judge in the reasoning behind his conclusions and convince him of their validity. As a result it is often necessary for an examiner to use charts and photographs to illustrate and explain his findings.

If the subject of testimony is particularly technical, the examiner can coordinate with counsel a line of questioning that will explain professional theory, then address the case at hand.

Juries pose unique problems in this area. Although most judges have a law school degree and should be able to grasp technical concepts that are properly explained, this is not necessarily the case with juries. It is best that each jury be assessed on its own, then decisions of approach be subject to decision between witness and counsel.

BIBLIOGRAPHY

Moenssens, André A. (1997). "Handwriting Identification Evidence in the Post-Daubert World," *UMKC (University of Missouri-Kansas City) Law Review*, 66(2): 251–342.

Risinger, D. Michael, Denbeaux, Mark P. and Saks, Michael J. (1998), "Brave New 'Post-Daubert World' – A Reply to Professor Moenssens," *Seton Hall Law Review*, 29(2): 405–490.

GRAPHOLOGY

Although there are some mentions of graphology as early as 1622 (Camilo Baldi, *Treatise on a Method to Recognize the Nature and Quality of a Writer from his Letters*), the practical origins of graphology are in the mid-nineteenth century, based upon the work and writings of Jacques-Hippolyte Michon (France) and Ludwig Klages (Germany). It was, in fact, Michon who coined the term "graphology" which he used in the title of his book, *The Practical System of Graphology* (1871 and reprints). The origin of the term "graphoanalysis" is attributed to M.N. Bunker.

Very simply, graphology is not Questioned Documents. The purpose of graphology is to determine the character of the writer; the purpose of a questioned document examination is to determine the identity of a writer. Thus, graphologists and document examiners cannot "trade jobs," since they are involved in very different skills.

There is a certain overlap between graphology and Questioned Documents, and perhaps therein is the basic misunderstanding. Some graphologists have suggested that psychological profiling can be the basis for writer identification. This is particularly the case in anonymous letter communications, disguised writing and forgery; although this approach can have investigative method, it is not valid for courtroom presentation.

The guideline here must be the method used. Questioned document methodology has been designed as a scientific procedure with one ultimate customer – the court. Not so for graphology! At best it is a psychological exercise poorly adapted to courtrooms. Nor is there any one graphological method. Various graphologists belong to various "schools of thought," thus wiping out any claim to accepted scientific method.

For many years there has been an ongoing debate in questioned documents circles about the validity of graphology. It cannot be denied that the psychological profile of the writer can have an influence on his handwriting, however it is not the function of this book to stray from the main point and consider to what extent that influence is to be felt or how can it be identified.

In Israel, very often document examination is rendered by the Hebrew word for "graphology." The basic point here is that we are talking about two entirely different disciplines which should not be confused. "Forensic graphology" is a contortion of words contradicting each other.

In summary, a graphologist represents a discipline not designed for the courtroom. Under no circumstance should a graphologist be considered an expert witness on questioned document matters.

BIBLIOGRAPHY – GRAPHOLOGY – CLASSICS

Klages, Ludwig (1897–1898), *Graphilogische Methoden*, Deutsche Graphilogische Gesellschaft, pp. 149–165.

Michon, Jacques-Hippolyte (1884), *Système de Graphologie*, Paris, 1884.

BIBLIOGRAPHY – GRAPHOLOGY – EVALUATION

Beck, Jan (1964), "Handwriting Identification and Graphology," *Journal of Forensic Sciences*, 9(4) (October): 477–484.

Beck, Jan (1967), "The Significance of Serious Graphology," Paper presented at the annual meeting of the American Society of Questioned Document Examiners, San Francisco, California.

CHAPTER 3

TYPEWRITERS

INTRODUCTION

The examination of typewritten documents requires a strong basis in the mechanics of typewriters. Before the examiner can properly examine the typewritten page, he must understand how the typewriter works, and how the document was produced.

It is true that typewriter mechanics also have a good understanding of the typewriter's operation (often better than that of the document examiner). The difference, however, is the thrust of their work. The mechanic wants to fix the typewriter. The document examiner wants to be familiar with the typewriter's operation only to understand the characteristics and individualities of the typewritten document that is produced, and not how to make the most cost-efficient repair in the shortest time.

When a document examiner receives an apparently typewritten document for examination, he must determine on which kind of typewriter the document was prepared. Different classes of typewriters have different characteristics and implications for the examiner. This chapter will, therefore, first explain the history of the typewriter. Then, the working principles of the various kinds of typewriters will be discussed. Within this background, questions of concern to the document examiner will be addressed.

In recent years computers and printers have replaced the typewriter in many businesses. Nonetheless, typewriters still continue to appear in Questioned Document cases as older documents and paperwork from lesser-developed areas are submitted for examination.

HISTORY

There were numerous attempts to invent the typewriter, beginning with Henry Mill in 1714. Generally, however, it is Christopher Latham Sholes (1819–1890) who is credited with having manufactured and marketed the first working typewriter or "writing machine." (In the nineteenth century the "type-writer" was the word used, in fact, for what we call today the typist.) Sholes was from

Milwaukee, Wisconsin, and he first demonstrated his machine in 1867.

Typewriters, though, were not quite ready for introduction into the commercial market on a large scale. It was not until 1873 that major marketing began. On 1 March 1873 Remington (a company manufacturing guns, sewing machines, and farming equipment) reached an agreement by which they added typewriters to their product list. One year later the first Remington typewriter was manufactured in the company's New York State factory. Another milestone of typewriter history was reached in 1881: at the YMCA in New York the first typing class was held with ten students.

These were the formative years in the typewriter industry. Different styles of machine were tried. There were different configurations of paper/key strike. There were even crescent-shaped keyboards that were used. In short, if anyone had a novel idea about typewriter design, there was usually someone willing to try it out. The machines developed might have been quite innovative, but in reality this entire period has only an interest of historical curiosity for today's document examiner.

By the turn of the century there were literally dozens of different companies trying to market their typewriters. In the ten-year period 1905–1915 alone, there were over 100 brands of machine vying for a place in the market. Some of these brands are a mere footnote to history (such as Yu Ess and Titania). Others, though, are still recognized in the second half of the twentieth century (Underwood, Smith).

As the typewriter developed, so did the layout of the keyboard. By the early part of the twentieth century, however, keyboards were standardized very close to what is being used today. The basic Latin character arrangement used almost worldwide is referred to as QWERTY (the order of letters in the second row from the top, naming the letters from left to right). Major exceptions are AZERTY, which is popular in France and QWERTZ in Germany/Austria on German language keyboards.

There have been concerted efforts to rearrange the keyboard based upon the "scientific" principles of mathematics and letter frequency. For all intents and purposes these efforts can be viewed as academic exercises with no real impact on the commercial market. Today there are new keyboards with a form to better accommodate touch-typing. This has no effect on the sequence of character keys. Again not dramatically affecting the basic letter layout, computer keyboards often have additional characters (e.g. the backwards slash "\" and keys for use on Windows).

By the time Hebrew and Arabic typewriters were introduced into the market, typewriter design was somewhat standard. The markets for these "foreign language" typewriters were too small for experimental typewriters.

On the practical level, if a document examiner receives a typewritten document for examination from the pre-1920 era, and he wants to know on what brand of typewriter it was prepared, how should he proceed? The answer is a very unscientific, "Good luck!" At this point in history Questioned Documents was itself in a formative era, and there were no developed systems to answer the question. By the time Questioned Documents addressed itself to the issue, a new generation of typewriters had already come on the market.

In those Western countries (such as United States, Canada, England, and Germany) where typewriter use has been historically more common than in Israel, the semi-modern period began in spurts in the mid-1920s. It is from that starting point that most Questioned Documents material on typewriting is based. In most of the Middle East typewriters first became relatively popular in the 1940s.

Since the advent of computer printers, the use of typewriters has steadily declined. Nevertheless, some typewriters will stay in use for years, and older typewritten documents will continue to be examined.

For many years typewriter manufacturers published extensive lists of serial numbers and corresponding years of manufacture. In the 1960s, however, that practice was discontinued when manufacturers decided that in publishing such statistics they were giving competition key data.

BIBLIOGRAPHY – EXAMINATIONS IN GENERAL

Nassar, Anwar Mohammad (1410 H–1989), *A Study on Typewriting* (in Arabic), Arab Center for Security Studies and Training, Riyadh, Saudi Arabia.

BIBLIOGRAPHY – HISTORY

Crown, David A. (1967), "Landmarks in Typewriter Identification," *Journal of Criminal Law, Criminology and Police Science*, 58(1): 105–111.

Jones, C. Leroy (Rocky) (1956), *History of the Typewriter*, Rocky's Technical Publications, Springfield, Missouri.

McCarthy, John F. (1973) "A Brief History of the Typewriter and Some Exemplars of Early Typefaces," Paper presented at the annual meeting of the American Society of Questioned Document Examiners, Silver Spring, Maryland.

BIBLIOGRAPHY – SERIAL NUMBER DATA

Schramm, Herbert F.W., *Liste der Herstellungsdaten deutscher undauslaendischer Schreibmaschinen*, Hans Burghagen Verlag, Hamburg (various editions).

MECHANICAL PRINCIPLES OF OPERATION

Although the name, key/bar typewriter, might at first sound technical and sophisticated, the reality is quite the opposite. These key/bar machines are nothing more than traditional "old-fashioned" typewriters. In fact, they are so "old-fashioned" that as of October 1979 one of the largest typewriter manufacturers, IBM, stopped making these typewriters. (In the 1980s IBM phased out of the entire typewriter line by ceasing manufacture of its "Selectric" line.)

The basic principles of operation of the key/bar typewriter are quite simple:

- The typist strikes a key on the keyboard.
- Through mechanical linkage or electric triggering, a type bar is thrown up from the type basket towards the platen.
- The typewriter is constructed such that a type block is mounted to the bar.
- The type block strikes the ribbon.
- The ribbon transfers the impression to the sheet(s) of paper behind it.
- The platen absorbs the force of the strike.
- As the key bar falls back into place, the carriage moves usually one unit to the next typing space, and the ribbon advances.

Sometimes the typewriter is designed to strike a character without advancing. This is called a dead key, and it is particularly common in typewriters designed for use with Romance languages having accent marks and for Arabic (hamza and tashdid). (Note: in many Arabic typewriters certain letters advance one unit, while others advance two units. In proportional spacing typewriters, the advance is usually between two and five units.)

One of the important differences between manual and electric typewriters is that on a manual machine the force with which a type block strikes the ribbon and the paper is a direct function of the force applied by the typist to the keys on the keyboard. Thus, a somewhat "uneven" strike is typical of many documents prepared on manual typewriters, particularly when the typist is inexperienced.

On an electric typewriter the typist merely triggers the mechanism of the typewriter to begin the process of imprinting the letter. Thus, since it is the typewriter mechanism which determines force, the end result is much more "even." (It should be noted that certain electric typewriters have been programmed to print character with "more" or "less" force. Typically, for example, a "period" would be printed with less force so as not to perforate the paper.)

In this discussion the ribbon was mentioned. Traditional ribbons can be made of cotton, nylon, silk or other fabrics, usually with various thread counts. Ribbons can also be available on traditional spools or in cartridges.

The ink vehicle on typewriter ribbons can be vegetable or animal (older). There is a wetting agent such as oleic acid, a wax, and glycol ethers. There are also pigments and usually blue or purple toners.

Generally, the text on these ribbons cannot be accurately retrieved if the ribbon has been used more than two or three times. Mylar and polyethylene ribbons come in single and multiple strike varieties; it is usually possible to read the text from a single strike ribbon. Sometimes sidelighting is needed to read the ribbon; this sidelighting can be accomplished by moving the light source or by moving its reflection through the use of glass or mirrors. In cases in which crumpling of the ribbon makes text retrieval difficult, one method is to sandwich the ribbon between glass plates to straighten it. (In some versions of an IBM Selectric, the general rule to read text is from the bottom row upward, then leftward to the next set.)

Speaking of typists, occasionally the question arises whether a document examiner can identify the work of a specific secretary. Although there have been cases where accurate identifications have been made based upon typing characteristics using manual typewriters (perhaps more accurately, typing quirks), these instances are more appropriate for curiosity articles and less desirable in actuality. When there is such an "identification" it should be made in carefully and concisely worded language.

Any attempt to identify/eliminate a typist based on the format of typed material (e.g. a letter) is a question of education, training and habit, if the document in question was routinely prepared. It is true that there are features of format which are very unusual, but only in the rarest of cases could they be deemed unique to only one possible typist.

After a letter is typed we have said that the carriage moves one typing space, but how much is that? First, one must differentiate between two classes of typewriters:

1   single space,
2   proportional (found only on electric models).

On a single space Latin character typewriter, all characters are allotted the same character width. Although there is no one industry standard, certain sizes have become popular. It is standard practice amongst document examiners to measure this character width, or pitch, in millimeters (mm) per character.

Category	mm per character
Micro	– 2.00
Elite	2.00 – 2.35
Pica	2.50 – 2.84
Macro	2.85 –

The size 2.12 (more exactly 2.11666, but generally rounded off) yields 12 characters per inch, and is popular in both Europe and the United States. Japanese companies have used 2.35, or 11 characters per inch. The United States pica measurement is 2.54, or 10 characters per inch. In Europe, 2.60 was popular, but it is now yielding to the American preference (particularly on typewriters manufactured for the business market). The Hebrew market has tended to prefer elite sizes. Unit spacing larger than 2.60 mm per character is rare in Latin characters (except for special purposes), but it is very common in Cyrillic typewriters, particularly those machines manufactured in the USSR (e.g. 2.80 and 2.83 mm per character). Numerous intermediate spacings have been used over the years, although today many of these are no longer being manufactured.

The introduction of the IBM Selectric II introduced the novelty of a typewriter capable to typing either 2.12 or 2.54 at the flip of a switch. This machine will be discussed in more detail in the section of single element typewriters.

Proportional typewriters were first field-tested in 1938 and released to the public in 1940 when IBM started to market its "Executive" model. In a proportional typewriter, horizontal spacing is divided into very small units. Then, each character is assigned a number of units proportional to its width. For example, the letter "i" can be given two units; "w" is often given five units.

Units Commonly Found on Proportional Typewriters

1/32 of an inch per unit

1/36 of an inch per unit

1/45 of an inch per unit

Thus far we have considered the horizontal spacing on a typewriter. Later on we shall see how a document examiner can learn from a typewritten document with which horizontal spacing it was prepared.

Each time the key bar falls back into the key basket after striking a letter, the character moves to the next space. As the typist continues, the carriage moves until the margin is reached (on the right side for Latin character typewriters, on the left for Hebrew and Arabic). Then, the typist must hit the carriage return to move to the next line. The distance between lines is called line spacing.

Common Line Spacing on Key/Bar Typewriters

8.00 lines per inch	certain micro fonts
6.00 lines per inch	many key/bar typewriters (common USA)
5.40 lines per inch	certain pica typewriters
5.28 lines per inch	IBM proportional typewriters

On most typewriters it is possible to select one of several line spacings. The most common settings are 1, 1.5, 2, or 3 line spaces. Many typewriters are also equipped with "free line spacing" whereby the typist can move the paper without removing the sheet from the typewriter. This is most commonly used for initial paper insertion and to align typing with spaces on a form. (Note that multiple sheets of paper and carbon can distort line spacing; the amount of distortion will be a factor of the number of sheets and their thickness.)

Motion is the distance the typewriter carriage or font segment moves when the shift key is pressed. Most common narrow motion measurements are between 0.260″ (6.6 mm) and 0.265″ (6.72 mm); the most common wide motion is 0.300″ (7.62 mm). Although most typewriter specimen forms include motion, very few examiners use this in their examinations today.

BIBLIOGRAPHY

Beck, Jan (1963), "Measuring the Shift Motion in Typewriter Identification," Paper presented at the annual meeting of the American Society of Questioned Document Examiners, Washington, DC.

Dreger, A.A. (1965), "Some Characteristics of Typewriter Ribbons," Paper presented at the annual meeting of the American Society of Questioned Document Examiners, Ottawa, Ontario.

Hilton, Ordway (1958), "Problems in the Identification of Proportional Spacing Typewriting," *Journal of Forensic Sciences*, 3(3) (July): 263–287.

SINGLE ELEMENT TYPEWRITERS

The name single element typewriter refers to those typewriters where all the font letters are placed on one piece of metal or plastic. This is usually done with the aim of being able to change the piece of metal/plastic, thus changing the letter style.

BALL ELEMENTS

Although there were several early model single element typewriters, the first commercially successful model was the IBM Selectric (Model 72) introduced on 31 July 1961. This typewriter was marketed in pica and elite versions. Then, in September 1971 IBM introduced the Selectric II with dual escapement (2.12 and 2.54 mm per character on the same typewriter). The Selectric family is undoubtedly the most popular and most successful "golf ball" element.

Selectric elements, a plastic base thinly coated with metal, are not easily manufactured. Several companies have tried with varying amounts of success. There are a number of primary sources for these elements: IBM, IBM World Trade Company (WTC), GP, CSA (wholesale sales to the trade only), and Brother. Examples of relatively short-lived companies which manufactured IBM-compatible elements are Camwil (specialty and custom-made), QWERTY, and Typerotor. Of these companies IBM manufactured a Hebrew element. Arabic (single unit spacing) was available from IBM-IBM/WTC and GP.

A word about IBM and WTC. Although these are divisions of one larger corporation, and although there is coordination in production and marketing, there are differences in products. For example, there are certain differences in typeface design between the IBM (Lexington, Kentucky) and WTC (Boigny, France) elements, even in the same basic type font. The two companies also assigned different forces of strike to certain keys based upon keyboard requirements.

Not all single elements are interchangeable. Several companies, such as Olivetti and Olympia, marketed their own unique products. (IBM also went through several manufacturing phases, which meant that certain older models and specialty products could not be used on all Selectric machines.)

Single element ball typewriters work on the principle of unit spacing coupled with the movement of the element. The ball both tilts upward/downward to ensure that the proper horizontal row strikes, and it rotates to select vertical column. A 180-degree rotation causes change between upper and lower cases.

On an IBM Selectric, the ball is seated on the mount with fastening accomplished by "teeth" around the lower circumference of the element and grooves in the hub. As a result, letters striking off center will not do so individually, but rather in horizontal line or vertical column groups. (It should be remembered that the pairing of a specific element with a specific mount causes these misstrikes. If either is changed – the element brought to another typewriter or another element is placed on the typewriter – a new pairing is made and generally no connection can be made to another pairing.)

DAISY WHEEL

These multi-spoked wheels which became popular in the 1970s work on the principle that a character is placed at the end of each spoke. The typewriter mechanism turns either clockwise or counter-clockwise, whichever is quicker, to select and print the appropriate letter.

Numerous companies have marketed daisy wheel typewriters. As with ball elements, different mountings have been used, and there is not always compatibility. Silver Reed has taken the matter of compatibility one step further. The daisy for their Hebrew (right to left typing) machine cannot be used on other Silver Reed typewriters.

Wheels are generally plastic, with no metal coating, hence they wear out much more quickly than coated ball elements. The primary indicator of a well-used wheel is character flattening and lack of definition, factors that can be of assistance in wheel identification. Some companies, however, have coated either single characters frequently used (e.g. period, comma) or the entire wheel (Diablo for Xerox).

The most widely sold Hebrew daisy wheels were manufactured by Qume (USA); they are compatible with IBM daisy printers.

Daisy wheels have been used on both typewriter and computer printers. Sometimes high-speed use, such as on computer printers, can cause drag, especially with the non-metal wheels. (Note that daisy printers for computers fall into the letter quality [LQ] category, but they are losing popularity because of slowness.)

BIBLIOGRAPHY – BALL ELEMENTS

Hilton, Ordway (1962), "Identification of the Work from an IBM Selectric Typewriter," *Journal of Forensic Sciences*, 7(3) (July): 286–302.

Hilton, Ordway (1973), "Identification of Work from a Selectric II Typewriter," *Journal of Forensic Sciences*, 18(3) (July): 246–253.

Levinson, Jay (1977), "The Interchangeability of Single Element Fonts," *Forensic Science*, 10(3) (November-December): 187–201.

Levinson, Jay (1979), "Single Element Typewriters," *Forensic Science International*, 13(1) (January-February): 15–24.

Miller, Lamar (1983), "An Analysis of the Identification Value of Defects in IBM Selectric Typewriters," Paper presented at American Academy of Forensic Science annual meeting, Cincinnati, Ohio, 1983.

BIBLIOGRAPHY – WHEELS

Beherendy, James E. (1988), "Class Defects in Print Wheel Typescript," *Journal of Forensic Sciences*, 33(2) (March): 328–335.

MAKE AND MODEL, TYPEFONTS

Very often the document examiner is asked, "On what kind of typewriter was this document prepared?" The question is phrased in terms of the typewriter used; however, the document examiner must first determine the style and manufacturer of the typefont. Only after he has made that determination can he address rephrase the question as: "On which typewriters is the typefont in question available?" To determine which font has been used is tedious work. However, with experience, hard work, and proper materials, an accurate determination can be made.

The first principle to be remembered is that there are many different styles of typefonts. Some people prefer decorative fonts; others prefer more simple type. For this reason manufacturers supply a broad variety. Latin fonts can be grouped into the following broad categories:

Font Category Description	
Monotone	The "traditional" typewriter font in which letters are with serifs
Courier	Numerous companies have "Courier"-like fonts
OCR	Optical Character Recognition.
	These fonts (OCR-A and OCR-B) are used for the optical scanning of a text. A common example is the encoding of bank checks in the United States
Script	As the name implies, a "handwriting-like" appearance in which letters are connected with each other
Proportional	All of those fonts used on proportional typewriters
Slanted	In these fonts the letters are slanted
Italics	As the name implies
Bulletin	Large type fonts used for readers with sight problems, speech makers, etc.
Micro	Extremely small typefonts for special uses
Specialty	The broad range of unusual type fonts made for special purposes

In Hebrew and Arabic there is not such a wide range of typefont available, although in recent years this has begun to change. In Hebrew the most traditional-looking font is an imitation of the printers' Aharoni type, although an italics font and a sans-serif have been on the market.

To assist the document examiner in identifying typefonts, there have been several published systems to examine the letter forms in typewritten documents and determine the style of font, make and model. (There have also been at least three efforts to computerize this information, the best known of which is Philip D. Bouffard's TYPE program.)

Today, some of these schemes are only of historical interest, since the information contained in them has been combined into later schemes.

BIBLIOGRAPHY

Schneeberger, W. (1944), *Die Schriftexpertise in der Gericht- und Anwaltpraxis*, Verlag Paul Haupt, Bern, Switzerland.

Gayet, J. (1949), "L'identification des marques de machines à écrire par les caractères," *Revue Internationale de Police Criminelle*, Interpol, Nos. 26, 27, 28.

A description of those schemes that are still in use as of this writing is included in Appendix II.

Each of these systems has its own particular benefits, and the examiner should not necessarily refrain from using more than one of the systems to check himself. All of the systems are based upon the same general working principle – the examiner must make basic differentiation decisions: size, shape of letters,

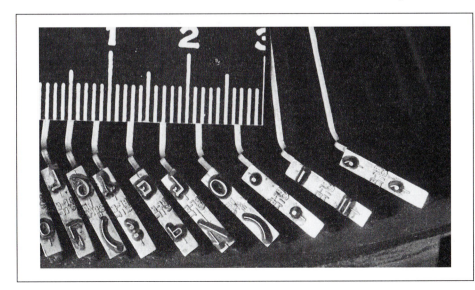

Figure 3.1

Manufacturer's symbol on font block (Courtesy of Israel Police)

etc. Typically, for example, the examiner would decide if the digit "4" has a triangular or open top, if the horizontal crossbar on the lower case "t" is symmetrical, or if the lower right tail of the lower case "a" falls off downward or curls up. By using enough of these characteristics it can be possible to arrive at the typefont used.

Once the examiner has determined the particular font used in the document which he is examining, he must then determine on which typewriters that font is known to have been used. The differentiation schemes listed above can be of help in determining this information. In many cases key dating information can be obtained (e.g. date of manufacturer's release, precluding earlier use).

When a document examiner issues a report concerning typewriter make and model, the proper language should be similar to this:

> The document in question was prepared on a typewriter equipped with RaRo (Ransmayer & Rodrian) monotone typefont and a unit spacing of 2.54 mm per character. This font is known to have been used on the following typewriters: /list/

The statement should almost always leave open the theoretical possibility that the font has been used on other typewriters, unless both font and typewriter are manufactured by the same source which does not engage in any "font only" sales.

It should be remembered that font slugs can be fitted to almost any typewriter. This is most obvious when looking at single element typewriters, since they are designed for the user to readily change fonts. Even on standard key/bar typewriters, however, it is possible for a technician to change fonts. This is most common when a customer requests special keys (e.g. foreign characters and accent marks, monetary symbols), though it should be pointed out that today, with the high cost of labor, this specialized service is not as common as it once was.

The specific case of the Hebrew typewriter provides an excellent example in which technicians, particularly in the Mandate and early State periods, often bought "blank" typewriters without characters, then they added Hebrew alphabet font as required. With older Hebrew typewriters, therefore, it is often very difficult to reconstruct on which machines a particular font appeared.

Although most typefont manufacturers took pride in the individuality of their product, there have been numerous examples (including Arabic and Hebrew) where there has been a conscious effort by one font manufacturer to imitate the product of another company. There are, therefore, cases in which differentiation between fonts is not at all possible. (This is particularly true of OCR fonts, where the entire purpose of the font is to perfectly duplicate a model design to best allow automatic reading and processing.)

BIBLIOGRAPHY

Mathyer, Jacques (1978), "Problem of the Identification of Typewriter Makes and Models," *Forensic Science*, Volume 11(1): 1–31.

Sources of Further Information
CSA http://www.quikpage.com/p/pck">CSA typewheels</A>
IBM http://www.uk.ibm/com/about/history2.html
Olivetti http://www.olivettilexikon.com/it/prodotti/scrivere/index.html
RaRo http://www.zim.com/rarotype

USING TYPEWRITER GRIDS

To determine the pitch or escapement on a typewriter, it is necessary to use a typewriter grid or measuring plate. These grids are usually boxes made in various measurements on a material which can be placed over a typewritten text. If this definition sounds complicated, an examination of Figure 3.2 will simplify matters.

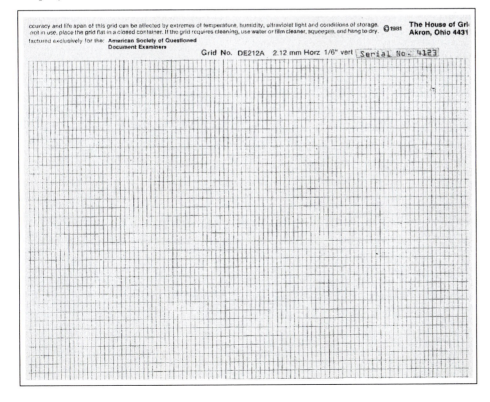

Figure 3.2

Example of a 2.12 mm per character (12 characters per inch) typewriter grid. This particular grid was made by special order of the American Society of Questioned Document Examiners in 1980. There are numerous grids available of various exactness standards.

In this case the examiner places the grid over his document to verify spacing. When each box on the grid is filled with a letter, then the examiner knows that he has made the proper measurement.

In theory this might sound simple, but it should be remembered that typewriters can have malfunctions where a letter or several letters consistently fail to strike properly. Particularly in cheaper typewriters there is also a manufacturing tolerance of spacing; that is to say that 2.23 need not be 100% exact. These individualities of the typewriter are covered in detail elsewhere. It is important at this stage, however, to remember that because of this factor it is always best to "home" the grid on one particular letter.

Tolerance in manufacture and rounding off the conversion of metric measurements to inches are not the only reasons that a pitch does not necessarily measure exactly. Machine wear can also be a factor. For example, a study of seventeen (17) IBM Model 72 (Selectric) typewriters was conducted, and the variation in the difference of pitch was found to be 0.0095 inch, presumably from use.

A critical factor in arriving at a proper measurement is the quality of the grid. This quality is based both upon the master and the copy being used. The master should, obviously, be made according to exacting measurements.

At one time it was thought that proper grids had to be etched on glass to prevent expansion in the heat; however, with modern technology, grids on film have become standard in the Questioned Documents profession. Care, though, should be taken to verify that film copies of grids are not enlarged or made smaller in the photographic process.

There are three basic types of typewriter grids: universal, specific measurement, and specialty. A *universal* grid has a range of measurements, so that an examiner can easily try several until he hits upon the measurement which he thinks is correct. Then, he should take the grid for that *specific* measurement and superimpose it over his document to verify his findings. This procedure is to be preferred over basing a conclusion on the universal grid, since it enables the examiner to measure the entire document all at once and not segment by segment.

Today there are certain typewriters which require a *specialty* grid for making measurements. The IBM Selectric II, for example, allows the typist to alternate between 2.12 mm and 2.54 mm by the flip of a switch. Thus, parts of a document can be typed with one pitch, while other parts are typed with the second pitch – without ever removing the document from the typewriter. A special grid for these cases has been developed with both pitches.

There are also specialty plates for proportional typewriters. These divide the typing line into units such as 1/32, 1/36 and 1/45 of an inch. The major problem in using these plates is that since the division is so small, it is sometimes difficult to see the spaces with sufficient clarity.

A short note about Arabic language typewriters. Most of the manual Arabic typewriters are built on a principle of one unit for certain characters, two units for other characters, and letter design which intentionally takes certain characters outside of their usually assigned spaces. Unfortunately, as of this writing there are no known grids designed specifically for Arabic.

An examiner using a grid in an Arabic language case should use a letter such as "b" or "f" for his base; if he needs a double unit to conform to the grid which he is using, he should use two of these letters printed consecutively. In Arabic cases use of a grid can be uniquely complicated, and knowledge at least of the alphabet is strongly recommended.

An examiner who measures the pitch in a typewritten document by ruler is not working as a professional or in accordance with the standard procedures accepted by the Questioned Documents profession.

There are document examiners who use line spacing measurements as a class characteristic to determine which make and model typewriter was used to prepare a document. Line spacing, or the space between horizontal lines of typing on a document, is best measured using a typewriter plate made for that purpose. In measuring line spacing, however, it should not be forgotten that many typewriters have settings for single space, single plus one half, double and triple spacing. Typewriters can also have a setting for "free spacing," allowing the typist to set line spacing according to his needs (usually used to adapt typing to spaces on forms). Since the "free spacing" is manually controlled, it can usually be spotted by a lack of exact line spacing consistency.

BIBLIOGRAPHY

Levinson, Jay (1974), "Arabic Typewriters," Paper presented at the annual meeting of the American Society of Questioned Document Examiners, Milwaukee, Wisconsin.

Millre, Lamar (1989), "Variations in Horizontal Spacing of IBM Selectric Typewriters," Paper presented at the annual meeting of the American Society of Questioned Document Examiners, Arlington, Virginia.

MAINTAINING SPECIMEN FILES

A key file for every document examiner handling typewriter cases is a specimen file. This will assist in verifying the identification of type font after a preliminary determination has been made using one of the schemes available. A well-constructed and maintained file will also allow the examiner to file dating information, changes in a particular font, and availability of a font on various typewriters.

Unfortunately, however, complete typewriter specimen files are not available from any central source. It is, therefore, the task of the examiner to collect specimens himself. (A by-product of this collection is greater familiarity with typewriters and their typed product, hence the work should not be automatically assigned to an assisting paraprofessional.)

The proper method for taking specimens is to use a standard format. The form in Figure 3.3 is a suggested model. This will ensure a more orderly collection once everything is filed.

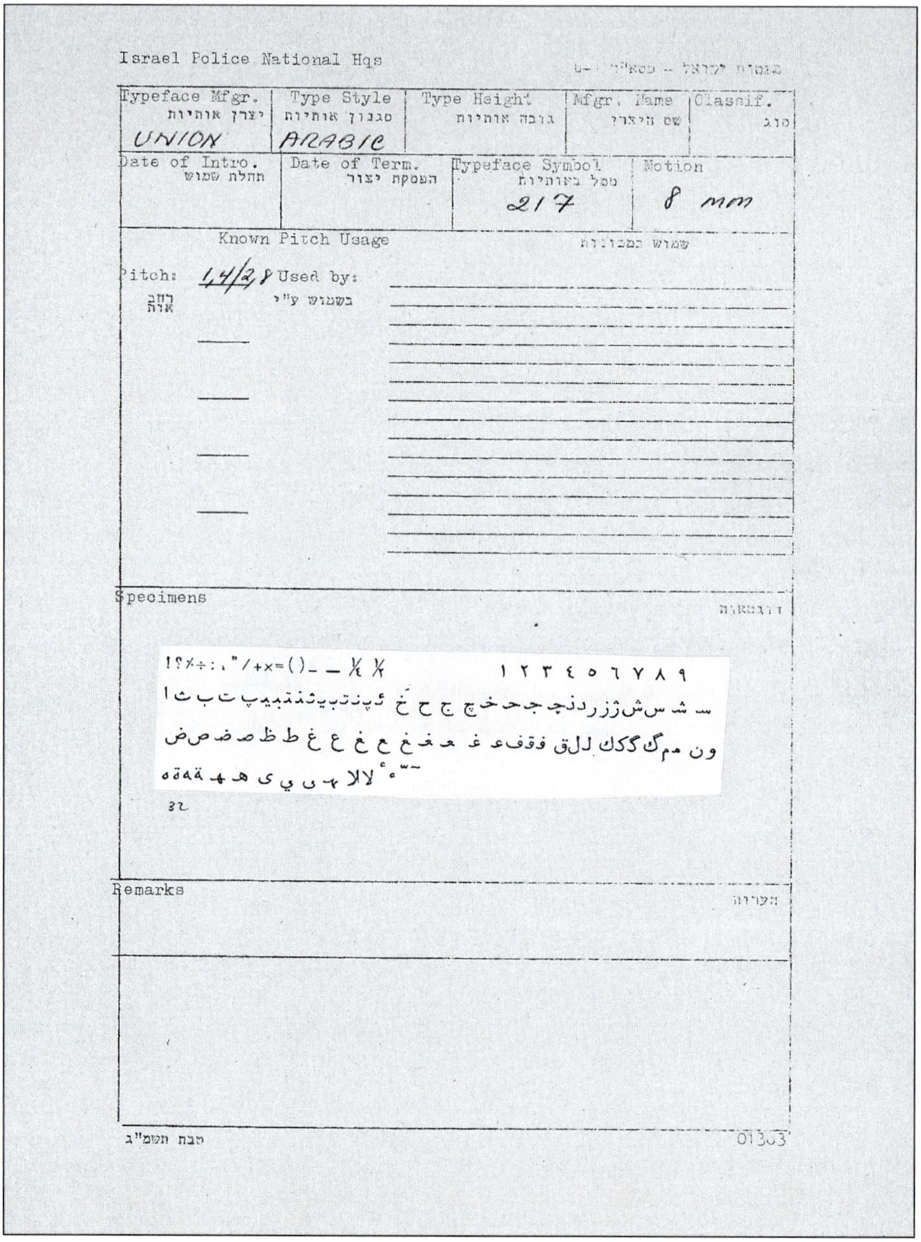

Figure 3.3

Specimen sheet in Arabic.

It is extremely important to record the typewriter name, model, and serial number on the form, and to write down the font symbol (to be found on the type block between the upper and lower case). A standard format sample, usually letters in the order of the keyboard, should be typed in upper and lower case. (It is recommended that one follow the Interpol format of striking every letter twice.) Some examiners conclude with a short sentence containing all the letters of the alphabet as shown.

```
THE QUICK BROWN FOX JUMPS OVER THE LAZY DOG.
       ~!@#$%^&*()_+{}:"<>? \

The quick brown fox jumps over the lazy dog.
       `1234567890-=[];',./ \
```

It should be remembered that on computers and single element typewriters, specimens should be taken for all available fonts.

For purposes of establishing the dates of font changes, the date of specimen and the examiner's name should also be added to the form. No specimen file is of any significant value if the pages are not filed properly. Filing should be according to the following categories in descending order: language, general style, pitch, font manufacturer and model, typewriter manufacturer, model, date of specimen. (An example of a filed item would be: Latin, monotone, 2.12 mm/char, RaRo 7, Hermes Baby [portable], 15 Dec 1970.)

The task of collecting specimens is quite time consuming and is undertaken without ever knowing if the specimen will actually be used. For this reason some examiners have relied on exchanging specimens with others. A note of warning: although it is very desirable for an examiner to collect type specimens as they appear in the advertising brochures of manufacturers, these do not replace actual specimens. Numerous manufacturers do not readjust their adverts after small changes in fonts are made.

BIBLIOGRAPHY

Crown, David A. (1982), "Organizing Your Typewriter Files," Paper presented at the annual meeting of the American Society of Questioned Document Examiners, Boston, Massachusetts.

TYPEWRITER INDIVIDUALITY

KEY/BAR TYPEWRITERS

So far we have discussed how to determine the make and model of a typewriter used to prepare a specific text. Obviously, if one has determined that a text was prepared with a font found on one make/model typewriter, and the suspect typewriter has a font of different manufacture, it is a clear conclusion that the suspect typewriter should be discounted. (Remember that the key item here is not the typewriter, it is the font.)

How does one proceed, however, if the class characteristics are the same? (that is to say, both the questioned text and the suspect typewriter have the same font). What are the individualities which will enable an examiner to say that a specific suspect typewriter was used to prepare your document?

At one time, when manufacturing and quality control standards were not as exact as they are today, there was barely a typewriter in use which did not have sufficient individualities to allow identification. These individualities generally included:

- letter damage (particularly to serifs)
- striking off center (high/low, left/right or a combination thereof)
- striking harder/lighter in certain areas

It should be noted that "abnormal" typing can distort and conceal typewriter characteristics. For example, "pounding" rather than typing can produce distortions significant enough to complicate (if not prevent) identification. For example, with excessive pressure the light areas of letters can print, shadows can appear, and there can be letter rebounds. Wide variations in typing pressure can create similar problems for an examiner.

Individualities in letters are not to be confused with machine malfunction, which can also help to identify a typewriter. Examples would be:

- broken "tooth" in the escapement bar
- malfunctioning margins
- defective platen

The correct procedure for an examiner to follow is for him to examine the class characteristics and individualities of his questioned document. Then he types out a specimen from the suspect typewriter and compares the results of his two examinations. It is a procedural error to "compare" questioned with specimen. For this reason Questioned Documents experts are called examiners – not "comparators".

When the question asked is if two documents were prepared on the same type-writer, the examination process is very similar. First determine the class characteristics of each document, then determine the individualities. Finally, compare the results of the two examinations.

השוואת האינדיבידואליות של המכונה

1 שיבוש חלקי באות:	6 סימן דר באות
2 שיבוש מלא של אות	7 סימן ממכת הפט"ש
3 נטיה של האות	8 צל ליד האות
4 קפיצה של האות	9 אות חסרה:
5 כיון סביב האות	10

ספרות וסימונים				אותיות גדולות				אותיות קטנות			
ד		מ		ד		מ		ד		מ	
?		1		ן		א		נ		א	
!		2		ן		ב		ו		ב	
.		3		ס		ג		ס		ג	
:		4		ע		ד		ע		ד	
;		5		ף		ה		פ		ה	
)		6		ף		ו		ק		ו	
"		7		צ		ז		צ		ז	
-		8		ץ		ח		ק		ח	
...		9		ק		ט		ק		ט	
'		0		ר		י		ר		י	
				ש		כ		ש		כ	
				ת		ך		ת		ך	
						ל				ל	
						ם				ם	
						ס				ס	

Figure 3.4

Form used by the Israel Police to record individualities on Hebrew typewriters.

In principle it can be possible in some cases to state without reservation that a particular document was definitely produced using a specific typewriter. (In professional terms, the number and type of individualities are such that they can be found on only one typewriter.) At what point can an examiner come to such a finding?

Over the years there have been numerous attempts to statistically analyze defects on Latin character typewriters. (The research projects listed in the bibliography were conducted on typewriters used to prepare texts in English. The results should be considered valid only for English because of letter frequency and keyboard layout. As of this writing, there have been no similar studies on Hebrew or Arabic typewriters.) While such statistical projects can be a definite aid in determining the frequency of a particular typewriting individuality, the reality is that long before statistical studies were undertaken, examiners were examining typewriter cases and drawing conclusions. Guidelines for the conclusions were always subjective, relying upon the experience of the examiner in typewriter cases.

Again a word of caution. There is variation in the operation of typewriters. This factor should be taken into consideration when making an examination.

The question has often been asked whether individualities in a typewriter can be "forged." The general answer is "no." There is, however, the controversial attempt at typewriter forgery in the Alger Hiss case in the United States.

SINGLE ELEMENTS

How can you tell if a document was prepared using a single element typewriter such as the IBM Selectric? The determination is critical as a prerequisite to identifying individualities.

In a properly functioning single element typewriter there will be even pressure on all characters. If the paper setting (on the IBM Selectric next to the element) is not adjusted properly, there can also be small "nicks" made by the background of the ball.

Malfunctions of single elements are rare. In most single elements any misstrike will not occur in a single character, but rather in an entire horizontal row or vertical column on the element.

One key in determining that a single element has been used is typefont identification, since there are differences between single element and key/bar fonts even when made by the same manufacturer.

BIBLIOGRAPHY – TYPEWRITER IDENTIFICATION

Gowdown, Linton (1962), "A Note on Identifying Typewriting," *Journal of Criminal Law, Criminology, and Police Science*, 53: 102–104.

Hilton, Ordway (1959), "The Influence of Variation on Typewriter Identification," *Journal of Criminal Law, Criminology, and Police Science*, 50: 420–425.

Hilton, Ordway (1963), "Kind and Number of Defects Necessary to Identify Typewriting,"

Paper presented at the annual meeting of the American Society of Questioned Document Examiners, Washington, DC.

BIBLIOGRAPHY – TYPEWRITER FORGERY

Tytell, Martin with Kursh, Harry (1952), "The $7,500 Typewriter I Built for Alger Hiss," *True*, 31: 17–19, 65–68.

BIBLIOGRAPHY – SINGLE ELEMENT IDENTIFICATION

Leslie, A.G. (1977), "Identification of the Single Element Typewriter and Type Element," *Canadian Society of Forensic Science Journal*, 10(3): 87–101.

Leslie, A.G. (1977), "Identification of the Single Element Type Ball to Typewritten Text," *Royal Canadian Mounted Police Gazette*, 39(4): 10–11.

TOY TYPEWRITERS

At one time, when typewriters were extremely expensive, cheaper toy typewriters were common, although their use was not a phenomenon that applied in most of the developing world. These machines were either of the typewheel or typebar varieties, and they were generally noted for substandard performance typified by letter rebounding and poor alignment.

BIBLIOGRAPHY

Wilson, Simeon (1963), "A Survey of Toy Typewriters, 1961," *Journal of Forensic Sciences*, 8(2) (April): 163–178.

CHAPTER 4

PRINTERS

INTRODUCTION

Since the 1980s computer-controlled printers have ceased to be restricted to data processing as personal computers (PCs) have increasing become popular. These printers have now moved with the PC into the home and general business office. They have become fast, simple, flexible, and popular and they have become a standard part of the caseload of questioned document laboratories. For the document examiner these printers can pose unique new problems which require an understanding not only of the printer, but of computers as well. They are also beginning to be versatile and multi-purpose, sometimes also serving as substitutes for duplicating machines.

PRINTERS IN GENERAL

Printers can be divided into two broad categories: impact (where a letter is printed as a result of striking the platen – such as single elements, dot matrix), and non-impact (such as thermal, laser, and ink jet). By the mid-1990s impact printers were being rapidly replaced by non-impact models.

There are numerous brand names of printers on the market. The printing mechanisms, however, tend to be made by only a few companies (e.g. Canon, Sharp, Okidata, Casio, Tokyo Electronic Corporation). These mechanisms are then sold for repackaging.

There has been a rapid development of printers and computers. The following rule must be remembered for non-Macintosh systems:

Operating System	Source of Font (1)	Source of Font (2)
CP/M	Printer character generator	Computer program
DOS	Printer character generator	Computer program
Windows	Windows	Computer program transferring the font into windows

Windows (in its various versions) is similar to the font generation process in Macintosh computers.

It is possible to add fonts to computer programs. In the Windows and Macintosh environment in particular numerous companies (totally unrelated to word processing or other software programs) offered font packages for sale. In the typewriter era fonts were typically designed from hand-made drawings. In the Windows environment fonts are generally made in one of two ways:

1   scanning from printed text of existing font;
2   design by the use of computer programs such as Fontagrapher®.

In dot matrix and older non-impact systems each size of font is designed separately. In Windows and Mac fonts there is one set of letters which is adjusted by computer for various sizes, bold and italics. A "family" of fonts is a term which describes a group of similar font weights and related features, such as light, bold, narrow, italics, etc. ("Bold" derived through Windows is different from a font designed as "Bold" [which can then be made "bolder" through Windows]). Note: there are computer fonts on the market which imitate older typewriter fonts.

Differentiating fonts made by different designers can be difficult if not impossible. Many traditional fonts have been imitated or re-designed by different sources. Sometimes the differences are so minute that they cannot be discerned, particularly in smaller sizes.

DOT MATRIX PRINTER

This is the most flexible kind of *impact* printing, allowing for a wide range of fonts and sizes. These printers are relatively inexpensive and enjoyed sales popularity in the marketplace in the 1980s.

A dot matrix printer is based upon a series of wire pins that strike the paper through a ribbon. These pins can be arranged in several configurations, the most common of which are:

Number of pins	Configuration
9	vertical column
9/9	2 vertical columns of 9
12	vertical column
12/12	2 vertical columns of 12
4/5	2 vertical columns (specialty)

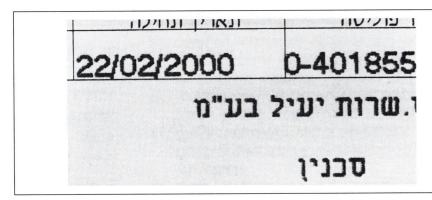

Figure 4.1

A 9-pin vertical column print head was used to fill in this car insurance certificate. There are seven pins on the base line and above. Two additional pins are below the base line.

Printing is accomplished by selecting the desired pins, pressing them against the ribbon, moving the print head, then repeating the process. On a typical 9-dot printer, for example, to print a capital "T," wire #1 (counting from the top) is imprinted. The print head is moved, and the action is repeated. The print head is again moved, and wires #1 through #7 are imprinted. Finally, wire #1 is imprinted two separate times. Wires #8, #9 are generally reserved for the lower loops of small letters such as "g," "y."

The above method is commonly known as draft quality. The resultant document from the average printer will be quite readable in terms of text, but there will be very obvious spaces seen to the naked eye between the printed dots. When a second (or third) printing is done with the paper moved ever so slightly, these printings fill in the empty spaces, and "near letter quality" (NLQ) is achieved. (Obviously, NLQ printing is much slower than draft, since it requires multiple printings of the same text.)

The wires themselves are very small. NEC, for example, reports a diameter of 0.085″ for pins arranged in vertical columns of 9. That diameter is reduced to 0.079″ for pins in vertical columns of 12.

The distance between pins is a variable, which is set by the manufacturer. To cite NEC again, the distance is 1/120″ with 9-pin columns; with 12-pin columns the distance is 1/180″. Okidata, on the other hand, uses a constant distance regardless of the number of pins in a column.

For all practical purposes these measurements might give a better understanding of how these printers work, however one could not expect a document examiner to base differentiation decisions upon such measurements. Accurate measurement of the distances is virtually impossible in printed documents.

In addition to the wires, each printer is equipped with a "character generator" (CG) regulating the design of characters (fonts). This is a computer chip, which dictates which wires will be impressed to form a letter. There is a wide range of CGs available, ranging from those with one basic font to those offering a choice of several. While the larger printer manufacturers also make their own CGs, there are companies which purchase CGs and affix them to their products. This situation is very much akin to typewriter fonts. Continuing this analogy, just as a document examiner identifies a typewriter font then the typewriters known to have been equipped with that font, so it is the case with printers. First the examiner must identify the CG, then he must list those printer makes/models known to have been equipped with that CG. (One should remember that many printer manufacturers use the same CG on more than one model.)

This is not a very simple situation. The CG in a printer is not as accessible as is the font in a typewriter, hence recording information on specimens is tedious work. Secondly, the CG can be bypassed by software in the computer. Simply, different fonts and escapements can be generated from computer programs. To cite one example, the popular font program, Letterix, can take a document created by any IBM-compatible computer word processing software and instruct a matrix or non-impact printer to print with a choice of numerous fonts, characters per inch, line spacings, etc. There are also options for italics, bold, compressed characters, etc. Many of the sophisticated word processing programs available today, particularly those offering a DTP (desktop publishing) capability, also offer their own type fonts (circumventing the CG).

The basic ramification is that once a document examiner has determined that a specific document was prepared on a dot matrix printer, he can try to determine the number of pins, but he will have difficulty making a meaningful "make and model" examination as he can with typewriters. The tool needed for such a determination is a chart of both CG and software fonts classified according to the number of pins involved.

Setting the earliest possible date that a document was prepared is a matter of determining CG and/or software release dates.

BIBLIOGRAPHY

Allen, M.J. (1987), "Dot Matrix Printers," *Forensic Science International*, 35: 283–295.

LASER PRINTERS

Although these printers have existed for many years, they have become popular only since the 1980s when new technology greatly reduced prices and made them affordable for routine office word processing.

The first of the "new" cheaper laser printers was Hewlett-Packard's LaserJet, based upon Canon's LBP-CX laser printer engine. The LaserJet works on a density of 300 dots per inch, thus giving high resolution to the resultant image.

The basic system is similar to many electrostatic photocopy machines, except that a laser is used instead of reflected light. Simply, electronic messages are transmitted defining characters according to dots in a matrix (a greater number of dots per inch [dpi] will cause better resolution). An electrostatically charged image is then formed on a drum or photoconductor. Toner of the opposite charge is attracted to the image, transferred to copy paper, then thermal bound. (There are some bi-component-type toners; magnetic carriers are used in the printing process, and they do *not* transfer to the paper. Hence, magnetic sensors will show the printed pages have no magnetic quality.)

Identification of a photocopier toner is usually of little practical value, since it is a class characteristic. In today's market, the various toners of different manufacturers are interchangeable.

BIBLIOGRAPHY

Brandt, James, James, Bruce and Gutowski, S.J. (1997), "Differentiation and Classification of Photocopier Toners," *International Journal of Forensic Document Examiners*, 3(4): 324–343.

Lee, F.L. Jr and Southmayd, Allen L. (1986), "A Look at the Laser Printer," Paper presented at the annual meeting of the American Society of Questioned Document Examiners, Savannah, Georgia.

INK JET PRINTERS

A.B. Dick introduced the first ink jet printer in 1969. IBM selectively marketed its Model 4640 after it was introduced on 20 January 1970; in June 1976 marketing of the machine started under the model number 6640. The working principle of the machine was that electrically charged ink was forced through a matrix and was sprayed on paper. The matrix was 40 dots high and 28 dots wide; the number of horizontal dots depends on the pitch to be printed. Each dot was 0.0006″ in diameter.

Although IBM phased out its original ink jet typewriter-style printer, several other companies market computer-attached printers working on very similar principles. These companies included Canon, Kodak and Epson.

By the mid-1990s most printers sold were ink jet of some sort. These printers can be grouped under the following classifications:

- *Continuous:* Electrostatic depositing of ink through a nozzle release.
- *Programmed inking:*
    - Thermal. Ink in cartridges is heated, causing a pressurized release.
    - Piezoelectric. "Solid" ink melted and pressure released onto paper where it again dries. This category can again be subdivided into direct release to paper and release to a wax-coated drum against which paper is rolled.

These printers use one or more of three types of ink cartridges: black, three color (cyan, magenta, yellow), four color (cyan, magenta, yellow, black). Doherty (1998) has put together tables listing types of printers with brand name/model numbers, cartridges, and relevant dates of introduction.

Modern ink jet printers use plain paper. In earlier models some used either plain paper, premium paper (with pigments and sizing agents to enhance quality), or clay-coated stock for better results.

BIBLIOGRAPHY

Doherty, Paige (1998), "Classification of Ink Jet Printers and Inks," *Journal of the American Society of Questioned Document Examiners*, 1(2): 88–106.

Masson, Jan F. (1979), "IBM 6640 Ink Jet Printer," Paper presented at the annual meeting of the American Society of Questioned Document Examiners, Rochester, New York.

CONDUCTING AN EXAMINATION OF DOT MATRIX

Proper examination procedure is to first set the class characteristics of the printer. If matrix, how many pins does it have? What is the printing mode? Draft? NLQ? Then, using a microscope or other magnification and a straight line as found on a typewriter plate, check the functioning of each pin. Does the pin strike properly? Is it in alignment?

The most commonly encountered printing malfunction in the experience of this author is the misalignment of a pin. In such a case the pin either does not strike, or it hits out of alignment. (Due to the small size of the pin and the intricate electronic mechanism, repair is almost always done by replacement of the entire pin column; Citizen, in fact, advertises "User-replaceable print head" on some of its models.)

Sometimes pin malalignment can be traced to poor manufacture of the vertical column in the print head. It is much more difficult to detect wear of the pin. When a printer is new, the pins have round heads. Through use these can become worn into different shapes. This fine detail on a very small surface, however, can be very difficult to identify, particularly through a ribbon.

Over-inking or uneven inking of the ribbon can also give the illusion of an irregular pin shape. This can be checked by looking for consistency each time the pin in question is struck.

Dot matrix printers can develop individualities, but their exact value in an examination can be difficult to assess. To date there is still no statistical study to assist an examiner in deciding the relative value of pins not functioning or striking properly. Does a leftward strike in Pin #5 and a rightward strike in Pin #6 mean that only one specific printer could have produced the document in question? For the time being these decisions are left to the intuition and experience of the examiner.

Not every malfunction is a potential individuality. Light striking of Pins #8 and #9 can be a class characteristic caused by poor alignment between the print head and the paper. A wavering horizontal base line or irregular line spacing can be indicative of poor paper feed.

It is often possible to determine what software was used to produce a right-hand justified text by examining spaces skipped to produce the end of line justification.

CONDUCTING AN EXAMINATION OF INK JET

Ink jet printers can be identified as a class based upon the lay of the ink on the paper and the unclean dotted nature of the font formation. Ink examinations are also possible to further define the class of printer with the potential of determining if printers using the same ink produced two documents[1]. These ink examinations fall into two overall categories:

- visual and photographic (filters, including ultra-violet, ultra-violet luminescence, FTIR and microspectrophotometry);
- chemical (TLC and possibly GC).

To date there is no system to find individualities in documents printed by ink jet printer.

CONCLUSION

The examination of texts produced by dot matrix printers does provide new challenges for the document examiner, but most of the principles involved are known from typewriter examination. The problem today is to apply those principles and to collect the specimen files needed.

SOURCES OF FURTHER INFORMATION

True Type Fonts	http://microsoft.com/typography/default.html
Monotype	http://www.monotype.com
Postscript	http://www.adobe.com/prodindex/postscript/overviewhtml
IBM Printers	http://www.ibm.com

[1] *There are at least three companies, Pelikan/Nu-Kote, Formulabs (Kimberly-Clark) and Reink, which produce ink for ink jet printers, and many of their cartridges are interchangeable on printers. Their products are also sold under a wide variety of commercial brands. The document examiner should take into consideration in his examinations that certain differences in ink do not preclude the possibility that two documents were produced on the same printer.*

CHAPTER 5

OTHER OFFICE MACHINES

FACSIMILE

Although the basic principles of facsimile (fax) have been used for many years to transmit news wire photographs, these machines first became popular in the late 1980s as transmission time was made significantly faster, coupled with a major drop in both purchase and operation costs. Today, a full-page document can be sent to any fax machine in the world in less than 30 seconds at the cost of a telephone call.

The principle of the facsimile is that the document to be transmitted is converted into analogous electrical signals. (It is possible that there be no original "document." When either an internal or external fax card is coupled with a computer, documents in the computer memory can be transmitted by fax. In these instances no hard copy need ever have existed.) These signals are transmitted by telephone from scanner/transmitter to receiver printer (more accurately, both the transmitter and receiver are transceivers).

There are numerous types of receivers/printers which produce the final product. In the case of a computer receiver, there again will be no hard copy document, unless the operator decides to send the incoming message to be printed.

The printers in a fax machine can be classified according to roll paper (being phased out)/cut paper, or according to printing methods (electrostatic, electrolytic, thermal, thermal transfer, etc.) similar to those found in many modern photocopiers. Faxed materials will have a "dot-like" appearance because of the digitalized transmission method. When faxed documents are sent to a computer, then to print, the printer will be that associated with the computer and not one unique to faxes.

Resolution of a fax is a factor of scanning lines per inch (lpi). On more sophisticated facsimile machines there will be several lpi settings.

Due to the use of thermal printing systems, fax paper is most often treated with lactone or fluorine chromogenic materials and phenol-type developers. In the case of thermal transfer methods, regular paper but with a thermal-sensitive ribbon is used.

It is generally agreed that fax copies do not have sufficient quality to provide a meaningful basis of examining handwriting, typewriting, etc., except in the case of blatant non-identifications.

Due to the relatively short time that fax machines have been used in the business world, there still remain major legal questions about the legal status of documents sent by fax. As a partial step toward legal acceptance, some fax machines place a mark on the original document, indicating that it was the actual model for the document sent. Other machines provide the sender with a microcopy of the document transmitted. Otherwise, the sender is left with a receipt showing that he sent "something," but he is hard-pressed to prove what.

In a fax transmission the telephone identification of the sender is often printed at the top of each transmitted page (in the United States this is required by law.) The fonts in that line are determined by the sending machine, hence examination of this line can be helpful in document source. There are also some fax machines which leave a distinct mark, often in a color which will not be seen in a photocopy, to record that the document has been sent by fax.

BIBLIOGRAPHY

Davidson, James and Tolliver, Diane K. (1992), "A Collection of Fax Fonts," Paper presented at the annual meeting of the American Society of Questioned Document Examiners, Milwaukee, Wisconsin, 1992.

PERFORATORS

Perforators are used to mark, cancel or register documents by cutting holes into the paper. Examples would be serial numbers in passports and identity documents, and the cancellation of checks and tickets.

Simple perforators make a single hole, sometimes of unique design, into a document. More sophisticated machines work on the basis of a grid, usually 4×6 holes (also common are 3×6 and 4×5), into which hardened metal pins are pushed. The paper is placed between the grid and the pins, thus causing holes to be cut.

There have been numerous attempts to forge documents whose fill-in includes use of a perforator. In the case of a standard perforator, the appropriate model can be bought on the commercial market. In cases of special order items, either a commercial perforator is used or the forger builds his own grid, usually with out-of-place and irregularly shaped holes.

Unless a very unusual or defective perforator is used, it is generally impossible to state that a specific (or genuine) perforator made a given set of holes. Rather, one must restrict him to a statement of "no differences were noted . . ."

The perforations on stamps are best measured using a standard philatelic gauge designed for collectors; such a gauge can be purchased in specialist phi-latelic stores. It measures both the size of the perforated hole and the number of holes per inch or centimeter. These measurements can be quite important in examining possible philatelic forgeries. Another historical use of a perforator in philately was to mark stamps designated for a specific purpose with a perfo-rated design; today this is a mere historical curiosity.

In the printing industry the dotted lines allowing for the tearing of one part of a document (e.g. a return stub or a coupon) from another part are often called "perforations." Once there was a specific machine that performed this function. Today it is an optional operation of a folding machine. These lines can vary in width and length. There is also variation in depth, however this is harder to control since (apparent) depth is a function of ink, paper and impression force.

BIBLIOGRAPHY

Levinson, Jay (1982), "Perforation Devices," *Forensic Science International*, 19(1): 1–10.

CHECKWRITER

Checkwriters are rather uncommon in Israel, but they are in use (particularly on bank checks issued in foreign currency). For many years they were found in most large offices in the United States. Now, however, computer-generated checks are replacing checkwriter machines.

The purpose of the checkwriter is to fill out a check in such fashion that alter-ations (and in some cases imitation) are impossible. This is done by imprinting on the checks and lightly perforating the paper; security is enhanced by using fonts, designs, or text not available on the commercial market.

A basic principle to be remembered is that the checkwriter is made up of both standard text (such as "the sum of") and variable text (digits, usually arranged on wheels). To take proper specimens from a checkwriter, a sample should be taken from all positions on the "sum" wheel, in addition to the impression of standard text.

There are checkwriters which do develop enough individuality as to permit identification.

Alteration of a sum entered with a checkwriter is possible, but it is quite difficult to perform, particularly when the checkwriter impression perforates the paper.

Another method introduced in the mid-1990s to limit check fraud is to have the cashier's register printer use a computer-generated program to fill in the check.

BIBLIOGRAPHY

Vastrick, Thomas W. (1979), "Checkwriter Identification," Paper presented at the annual conference of the American Society of Questioned Document Examiners, Rochester, New York.

Vastrick, Thomas W. (1980), "Checkwriter Identification II Individuality," Paper presented at the annual meeting of the American Society of Questioned Document Examiners, Vancouver, British Colombia.

PAPER CUTTERS

Although this is not a very sophisticated piece of equipment, it does afford the document examiner with the possibility of an examination. There can be defects in the blade of a cutter which can be seen in the paper it cuts. This is most evident in a large cutter used for multiple sheets of paper. There have been instances in which it was shown that one group of pages was cut on the same machine as another group.

COMPUTERS

Initially it might seem strange to include the computer as an office machine of interest to questioned document examiners, since it requires an output device such as a printer to produce a hard copy document.

- First, one should remember that we are moving into a "paperless" era in which documents of significance (hence possibly forged) need not necessarily be produced in hard copy. To cite just one example, it is now possible to order a wide range of products, from books to airline tickets, via the Internet and e-mail with payment made without producing a hard copy document.
- Second, computers store information, such as previous drafts of documents and "erased" segments, that might well be of interest to document examiners.

There is still insufficient experience to determine which aspects of computer fraud are best handled by document examiners and which by computer experts. Retrieving "erased" text from the computer hard disk or from a diskette is probably done best as a coordinated effort between the computer expert, to obtain the text, and the document examiner, to assess its importance in the case being examined.

BIBLIOGRAPHY

Noblett, Michael G. (1996), "Unintended Consequences from Documents Prepared Using Word Processor Software," Paper presented at the annual meeting of the American Society of Questioned Document Examiners, Washington, DC.

Sources of Further Information – Ink Jet Printers and Inks

Canon	http://www.canon.usa.com
Epson	http://www.epson.com
Hewlett-Packard	http://www.hp.com
Lexmark	http://www.lexmark.com
Nukote	http://www.nukote.com
Okidata	http://www.okidata.com
Xerox	http://www.xerox.com

CHAPTER 6

CACHETS AND SEALS

CACHETS

Although most cachets are usually called "rubber stamps," the reality is that they can be made from a number of different materials. In general, a soft and pliable plastic ("rubber") is mounted on a thin cushion, giving a clear impression under most circumstances. For various reasons (e.g. security, constant use), however, other materials (including hard metal) are also used.

A frequent class characteristic of a "rubber" cachet can be the dotted/porous nature of the rubber under heavy magnification. Metal cachets often show uneven distribution of ink.

Individualities can include cut marks when separating the cachet from a larger sheet and points of wear.

It is very possible to produce a forgery of a cachet. This can be accomplished by photographing a cachet and making a new one from the photograph. It is, therefore, very difficult for an examiner to authenticate a cachet; made either by setting type to imitate an existing cachet, or by photography. Unless there are careless errors made by the forger, the examiner has to resort to a statement that no evidence indicative of forgery has been noted (not confirming authenticity).

In 1996 Brother introduced the SC-100 flat die cachet, followed two years later by Model SC-2000 Stampcreator and Model SC-300 adaptable to personal computers, in which thermal transfer is used in conjunction with a porous inking pad to transfer images. SC-2000 cachet impressions are 600 dpi, which produces good line resolution and even/strong inking. The SC-300 tend to have weak inking inside letters.

BIBLIOGRAPHY

Herkt, A. (1985), "Rubber Stamps: Manufacture and Identification," *Journal of the Forensic Science Society*, 25(1): 23–38.

Kelly, Jan Seaman (1998), "Flat Die Stamps: A New Technology from Brother," *Journal of ASQDE*, 1(2): 82–87.

Levinson, Jay and Perelman, Benjamin (1983), "Examination of Cachet Impressions," *Journal of Forensic Sciences*, 28(1): 235–241.

SEALS

Most dry seals are made from sandwiching the object (recipient of the seal) between male/female versions of the seal cut in hard plastic or metal and applying pressure. Use of these seals varies from authentication of a document to "tying" a picture to a passport (by impressing part of the seal on the document and part on the photo).

In most cases these seals are difficult to read, particularly when a thick or multi-page object is involved. Many forgers rely upon this fact and produce semi-legible impressions. In this spirit, the most common substitute in a forgery for a real dry seal is an impression taken from a coin.

The two most common methods to read a dry seal are oblique lighting and shading with a pencil. In the latter a thin sheet of tracing page is placed over that side of the object page where the impression is raised; the impressions are then shaded with the side of a pencil. (This method has the fault of possibly causing damage to any indented writing present but not visible to the eye.)

In a wet seal a hot material such as wax (traditional) or plastic (modern) is placed on a surface (usually the flap of an envelope). A female seal made from metal is placed in the hot material, then it is removed. The seal is ready when the hot material dries.

Wet seals are not particularly secure, and passable forgeries do not require major skill to produce.

CHAPTER 7

PRINTING

INTRODUCTION

It is often very important to establish the method by which a document was printed. This is particularly significant in the case of security documents and currency, where the method of printing is a basic part of the security of the document. Even in other documents, however, this question can be important.

United States dollars, for example, are printed by intaglio (a type of engraved printing) with serial numbers entered by letterpress. Any deviation from this process, such as printing by photo offset, is a conclusive proof of forgery.

HISTORY

The era of printing is often said to have begun in 1440 when Johann Gutenberg (c. 1400–1468) assembled the first printing shop using moveable type. Thirty-five years later the first book was printed in moveable Hebrew type. The art remained more or less the same until the late eighteenth century when parts of the wooden printing presses were replaced by metal. The truly modern era began with two inventions:

1   the invention by William Church in 1822 of a "fast sort" machine capable of sorting 3000 pieces of moveable type per hour, and
2   the introduction of the rotary press in 1866 (roll-fed paper was printed on both sides at the rate of 25,000 per hour).

METHODS

Today there are numerous methods of printing. How is the document examiner able to look at a document and determine the method of printing?

First the document examiner must understand each of the various printing processes used and the "tell-tale" signs which they leave behind on a document. Then he can examine his questioned document to decide which process was used.

Printing can be divided into three major categories depending on whether the printed surface is depressed, flat, or raised: relief (letterpress), plano-graphic (lithography, offset), intaglio (gravure, rotogravure).

LETTERPRESS

From a very simplified point of view, a text is set in type, ink is placed on the letters, then the letters are pressed against a sheet of paper. From the document examiner's perspective, the result is that the pressure involved leaves a slight indentation in the paper, and small quantities of excess ink tend to accumulate along the "walls" of the indentation.

Over the years there have been changes in letterpress, although the basic principle has remained the same. At first, most texts were set with single letter moveable type, but as time progressed, this began to change. One of the most important changes in this regard was the invention of the linotype machine by Ottmar Mergenthaler (1854–1899) in 1884. This enabled the typesetter to enter a line of type, then "send" the text to molding, from which he received a block of text. These blocks of text were then fastened together to constitute pages, and documents were printed using the letterpress method. When the blocks were no longer needed, they were melted down. Today, this method of printing is in decline.

As the popularity of letterpress grew over the years, the variety of available type styles increased. In some questioned document examinations it is important to determine if a particular printer does or does not own the style font with which a document was printed.

Another major change in letterpress has been the materials used for printing. Once, all type was metal. Today, however, hardened plastics have been intro-duced.

When plain text is printed by letterpress, the raised letters have a flat surface to which the ink will be applied. For pictures the image is made in a series of dots; the greater the concentration of dots, the darker the image will be.

There are several methods used to make letterpress plates: (1) materials such as copper, zinc or magnesium can be etched, (2) a photographic exposure can be made on a specially treated plastic plate, then unexposed areas are removed by washing, or (3) metal or plastic can be engraved with an electronically con-trolled stylus. These plates are then printed in either flatbed or rotary format; in flatbed the plate is flat, in rotary it is curved to fit the roller.

The letterpress method is an industry standard, but it has slowly been overcome by other processes. The main use of letterpress today is to enter serial numbers and perform special tasks such as the printing of perforations or tear lines.

PHOTO-OFFSET

Formally known as offset lithography, this was started by Rubel in 1904. This is the most common method of printing today, and the equipment required is quite compact. Simply, an electrostatic image of a document is transferred to a specially treated plate, then the plate is preserved through a process of heating and the application of chemicals. The plate is placed into a printing press which works on the principle that water will not mix with oil-based ink. Thus, ink is received by the image on the plate, and it is rejected in the non-exposed areas that receive water. The ink is then transferred to a second (soft) roller which will come into contact with the paper and print.

For a document examiner, the key point is that the plate never comes into direct contact with the paper. As described, the plate leaves an impression on a roller, and the paper touches the roller. The results are that the ink "takes" to the paper absolutely smoothly, and there is no indentation as found in letterpress. The ink tends to feather slightly at the edges of the letters. (It is very rare to be able to conclusively determine whether the electrostatic plate was made from a plastic or from aluminum, although from the printer's perspective the difference is significant.)

One major pitfall for the document examiner should be remembered. If a document has the illusion of indentation, but there is no actual recess in the paper, the examiner should take into account the possibility of a document originally printed by letterpress, then printed a second time by offset. In such a case the camera often photographs some of the letterpress characteristics. (As a matter of fact, many printers produce their model text by letterpress, then they make further copies by offset printing, although now this procedure is yielding to a computer-generated "original.")

ENGRAVING

Also known as intaglio. Yet another basic method of printing is to engrave, or cut, an image into a plate. The first recorded use of this process was by Tommaso Finiguerra in 1252. In the United Kingdom the first postage stamps were printed in intaglio by Rowland Hill in 1838.

The basic characteristic in the resultant document will be "raised ink" resting on top of the printed sheet. There is a difference in printing according to the material in the plate used. Steel, for example, gives a much sharper image with better ink flow than copper. Therefore, an expert document examiner will frequently be able to identify the type of engraving plate by examining its work product.

Offshoots of these methods are photogravure (invented by Klietch in 1910) and rotogravure.

OTHER

There are other methods of printing, however these three described above account for the vast majority of business documents and security papers to be found today.

PRINTING INKS

Using the proper ink is a key aspect in printing a document, and not all inks can be interchanged between every printing process.

The most common printing ink is black. When a document examiner wants to determine if two black printing inks are similar, he can use several procedures, the most popular of which are: TLC, HPLC, GC, GC-MS, microspectrophotometry, electrophoresis, and energy dispersive electron microscopy. (It should be remembered that an analysis of the ink-on-paper should be made, from which an analysis of the paper-without-ink is to be subtracted.)

EXAMINATION POINTS

A trained document examiner can learn much from a printed document. In offset, for example, the examiner can sometimes determine if two copies of the same document were printed from the same plate. (This is done by looking for "photographic dirt" which was not removed from a negative before it was transferred to the plate before printing.)

Both ink and paper have a strong influence on printing. Hard paper, for example, will not accept graphics as readily as softer paper.

Font can also be an important aspect of an examination, since it can be a point to differentiate a genuine document from a forgery. Although many fonts are very similar, small differences can often be found between different manufacturers. Printed resources to identify fonts are listed in the Bibliography. In addition there are computer programs connected with scanners, such as FontFinder™. It should be remembered that these computer systems suggest fonts to the examiner; they do not determine the font used"[1].

It is also important to look for signs of document restoration. If, for example, a genuine document is made out in someone's names, that name must be erased before the document can be used as the basis of a photo offset forgery. If the name has intersected text or a line, those must also be restored. Signs of restoration can be indicative of this process.

[1] This is the same principle on which the Morpho Automated Fingerprint Identification System (AFIS) is based.

BIBLIOGRAPHY – GENERAL

Beck, Jan (1967), "Printed Matter as Questioned Documents," *Journal of Forensic Sciences*, 12(1): 82–101.

Durrant, W.R., Meacock, C.W. and Whitworth, R.E. (1973), *Machine Printing*, Focal Press, London.

Lacy, Lucile P. (1957), "Modern Printing Processes," *Journal of Criminal Law, Criminology and Police Science*, 47: 730–736.

BIBLIOGRAPHY – FONTS – ENGLISH

Apicella, Vincent, Pomeranz, Joanna and Wiatt, Nancy (1990), *The Concise Guide to Type Identification*, Lund Humphries, London.

Atkins, Gordon (1975), *The Classification of Printing Types*, Apple Barrell Press, Leicester, England (limited edition).

Karch, R.R. (1952), *How to Recognize Type Faces*, McKnight & McKnight, Bloomington.

BIBLIOGRAPHY – FONTS – HEBREW

Spitzer, Moshe (ed.) (5750 – 1989–1990), *The Eternal Alphabet: Collection of Articles Dedicated to the Development of Hebrew Fonts* (in Hebrew), Publications Department, Israel Ministry of Education and Culture, Jerusalem.

Tamari, Ittai (1985), *New Hebrew Letter Type*, University Gallery, Faculty of Visual and Performing Arts, Tel Aviv University.

DESKTOP PUBLISHING (DTP)

During the late 1980s and the 1990s desktop publishing developed parallel to the personal computer. In DTP the system operator needs:

- *Input devices:*
  - Keyboard and mouse
  - Information libraries (such as drawings and pictures on computer diskette (optional)
  - Scanner (OCR or more popularly digitized) (optional)
- *Processor:*
  - Computer and appropriate software
- *Output devices:*
  - Printer
    or
  - Connection to off-site printer (modem)

The development of this technology has revolutionized the printing industry, and it has brought publishing literally into the home. These developments have also made life easier for the forger.

Desktop publishing can produce several different types of forgeries with relative ease compared with older methods:

- Notional documents. Impressive looking documents such as different types of certificates can be produced.
- Copies of authentic documents. This includes originals produced through DTP as well as forgeries created through use of a scanner.

The digitized graphics scanner, in particular, has enabled the rapid reproduction of documents with the possibility of cleaning or "doctoring" the pictures through computer software (e.g. PhotoShop®).

Not every personal computer user can use DTP and certainly not to the level of creating forgeries. Extensive training is required to master all of the nuances involved in producing a quality reproduction of a sophisticated document. That training, however, is readily available to all those who buy computer books or who enroll in computer courses.

CHAPTER 8

DOCUMENT COPYING

PHOTOCOPIERS

The first primitive photocopier was introduced in 1938 by Carlson, but it is only since the 1960s that photocopiers have been the primary method of making copies of documents. These replaced standard photography which was time consuming and much more expensive.

Photocopiers can be categorized into black and color, then again into the following major groups.

MONOCHROME (BLACK) PRINTERS

- *Indirect electrostatic* (plain paper). This system is perhaps best known by the popular name, "xerography." A selenium coated surface that will hold an electrostatic charge is given a positive electrostatic contact. After exposure to the document to be copied, negatively charged toner clings to the copy paper by positive–negative attraction in those areas where an image is to be retained. (Toners can be dry or liquid [no longer in common use], and they can often be differentiated under magnification; when they are liquid, they adhere to the page by either blotter or dry fusion.) Although the basic technology has been standard for a number of years, there have been numerous changes in the chemistry of toners and in fusing techniques. Toners generally contain a binder, pigment, a carrier and additives to prevent caking and give polarity. Color copiers work on the same basis. Color is determined by the proportional use in the toner of the four basic colors.

  Efforts have been made to determine the manufacture of photocopiers based upon the toner used. This can yield results for OEM (original equipment manufacturer) toners, but non-OEM products complicate the issue. There are also several companies that have marketed different types of toners. This is true for both black and color toners.

- *Direct electrostatic* (coated paper). This is a very similar system through which the image is transferred directly to the copy paper without use of transfer from an intermediate surface.

- *Thermography.* Although no longer popular, this method started in 1950 under the 3M trade name, Thermo-Fax. A special paper with a ferric compound stored in a polyvinyl binder is exposed to the document to be copied using infrared radiation. One major problem with the system is that the treated paper tends to flake and break after a period of time.

- *Dual spectrum.* A thin coated intermediate sheet becomes decomposed with light, leaving material in the order of the document to be copied. Chemicals on the copy react to form a permanent image.

- *Diazo.* A transparent or translucent document to be copied is placed facing sensitized paper with a diazonium compound. Ultra-violet light is exposed, causing a chemical reaction which leaves a dye in the image area.

- *Diffusion transfer.* In a scenario similar to standard photography, a sheet containing silver halide together with other chemicals is exposed to light. It is paired with a non-light sensitive second sheet lined with gelatin. The document to be copied is put in contact with the first sheet, and light is supplied. The silver halide preserves a negative image, which is then put in contact with positive paper. This method was reportedly first applied to photocopiers in West Germany in 1948.

- *Dye/gelatin transfer.* The document to be copied is exposed to a light sensitive matrix (containing unhardened gelatin with silver halide, a tanning developer, and a color compound) using reflex lightening. The matrix is placed in an alkaline solution which begins the chemical process by which the negative matrix image is transferred to paper, resulting in a positive image.

- *Stabilization.* Here the silver halide is converted into metallic silver in areas without an image to be retained, thus leaving a negative after processing (with text on black background). After stabilization of the image this negative can then go through the same process to provide positive copies.

Office equipment is a very competitive market, and in recent years there have been frequent changes in the industry. Coated paper (usually zinc oxide) copiers, for example, have become a rare item. Sheet-fed machines have also become much more popular than roller-fed paper supply.

Some photocopiers do not copy material that is very close to the edge of the paper.

Although the quality of copiers is constantly improving, these machines still are not perfect. In some machines, for example, a 1:1 copy has been off by as much as 3%! (Document examiners can avail themselves of computer programs to eliminate by intentional and system-generated size difference as well as vertical or horizontal shrinkage/expansion.)

COLOR COPIERS

3M introduced the first color copier in 1969. This was followed by the Xerox color photocopier (Model 6500 introduced in New York City on 23 May 1973 and marketed nationally in 1974) which works on the indirect electrostatic principle, using color toners. These were two of the first color copier on the market, though today there is considerable competition. Only in the 1990s, after vast improvements in the product accompanied by lower cost, did these machines see wide use.

Color copiers can be classified as *electrophotographic* (laser) (using toners), *photographic* (silver halide process on photo-sensitive paper, usually zinc oxide), *cylithographic* (microcapsules called cyliths are exposed to light), and "drop on demand" *ink jet* (based upon three or four basic colors). Imaging can also be digital or analog. (The trend is decidedly away from analog to digital images in both monochrome and color machines.) Depending on the make/model in question four colors are imprinted on documents in sequence or in individual passes; some color copiers use black as one of the four colors, while others use black only for monochrome copying.

Another approach has been to classify color copy machines according to the TLC, IR, UV, or luminescent characteristics of their toners. Color photocopiers made in Japan have machine-specific patterns that appear in UV in documents copied *when the company-supplied toner is used*. This approach has not taken into account manufacturing differences over a span of time and products made for sale by other than the owner of the product label. The current interchangeability of products severely limits this method except in countries with limited or relatively closed markets.

In a number of countries color copiers have been used to "counterfeit" local currency. A question often arising in court is whether such a forgery is truly of a quality that it can fool the public. The answer very much depends upon the citizen looking at the currency. One fact, however, is quite certain – determination of forgery accomplished by using a color photocopy machine should provide no real challenge to a document examiner; however, that is certainly not to say that the average citizen has the same skill.

In very basic terms it can be said the laser-type color copiers produce images by layering toners of three and four colors. Ink jet copiers also use three or four colors, but they are not layered and they tend not to splatter out of place.

BIBLIOGRAPHY

Doud, Donald (1976), "Some Characteristics of Xerox Color Reproductions," Paper presented at the annual meeting of the American Society of Questioned Document Examiners, Atlanta, Georgia.

Hokkand, Neil W. (1984), "Photocopy Classification and Identification," *Journal of the Forensic Science Society*, 24: 23–41.

James, Elizabeth L. (1987), "Classification of Photocopy Machines by Physical Characteristics," *Crime Laboratory Digest*, 14(2): 54–73.

Kelly, James (1979), "Copying Processes," Paper presented at the annual meeting of the American Society of Questioned Document Examiners, Rochester, New York.

Seiger, Danielle Pettine (1997), "Differentiation of Documents Produced Using Color Output Technologies," *Crime Laboratory Digest*, 24(1): 10–14.

Stimpson, T.A. and Ostrum, R.B. (1992), "A Study of Class Characteristics of Modern Office Production and Reproduction Technologies," Paper presented at the annual meeting of the American Society of Questioned Document Examiners, Milwaukee, Wisconsin.

EXAMINATION OF PHOTOCOPIED DOCUMENTS

Very often a document examiner is queried whether he can examine a photocopy. To be certain, there are basic limitations to such an examination. Such examinations, however, should not be automatically discounted[1].

With the increased quality of modern photocopies there usually is enough detail to conduct a major portion of an examination. The examination, though, should be systematic and cautious. As a precaution against false information the examiner should scan the basic document. Is the toner (or equivalent material) evenly spread? Are there any noticeable machine defects? Is there loss of detail in the corners? Can the true size of the original document be established? Once these questions have been considered, then the examiner is in a better position to conduct his examination.

Another factor that should be taken into consideration is "generation." Photocopies do lose a certain amount of detail. In a first generation photocopy this loss of detail might amount to little more than an annoyance, but by the third or fourth generation copy the loss of detail might already preclude an examination. Thus, it is always best to examine the earliest generation photocopy possible.

As anyone familiar with photocopies will realize, the finer a detail in the original, the less chance it will be recorded in a photocopy. This is particularly true when speaking about weight of pressure or impression, a very light trail connected with a pen lift, or a slightly damaged serif. This is part of the reason why some examiners prefer not to render absolute conclusions in photocopy cases.

Photocopies also invite alteration. Pasting in a signature, or even an entire paragraph, is obviously easier to do in a photocopy than in an original document.

If the document examiner is able to determine the class characteristics of make/model, he can then use date of introduction information to set the earliest date possible.

[1] *In Case T/P (Jerusalem) 373/86 State of Israel v. Ivan (John) Demjanjuk the defense argued that document T/149 was examined in photograph and not as an original, hence the examination results should not be introduced into evidence. The Court denied this contention.*

BIBLIOGRAPHY

Hilton, Ordway (1977), "Can Typewriting Be Identified from Photocopies?" Paper presented at the annual meeting of the American Society of Questioned Document Examiners.

Scott, Charles C. (1984), "Handwriting Instrument Questions: Opinions Based upon Photocopies," Paper Presented at the annual meeting of the American Society of Questioned Document Examiners, Nashville, Tennessee.

IDENTIFYING A SPECIFIC COPIER

Frequently a document examiner is called upon to determine if two documents were copied on the same photocopy machine.

The first step in any such examination is to determine that the photocopies in question were produced on the same class copier. In making this determination it should be remembered that a difference in toner can indicate that the second document photocopied could have been produced on the machine that made the first, only after the machine was filled with another batch of toner.

Through the 1970s a number of copiers could be identified by the grip marks or trash marks which they left on photocopies; although these machine class characteristics still do exist, they have become much more difficult to find. The basic place to inspect for grip marks is usually within 0.5″ of the edge of the page. An alternative method is to find indications of unique fusion marks on the photocopier roller.

Another method is to look for the photocopying of scratch marks on the glass plate over which the document to be photocopied is placed. These marks will always show up in the same place if the photocopy is done 1:1. If the document's photocopies are increased or decreased in size, calculation should be made to determine the location of the scratch.

A "wandering" scratch is often indicative of damage to the drum. In such a case the scratch will reappear at consistent intervals depending on the size of the drum.

OTHER DUPLICATORS

It was once not cost-effective to use a photocopy machine to duplicate a large number of copies of the same document, yet time and cost also prohibited use of classic photographic techniques. For this reason an "office reproduction industry" developed, offering options that are, today, usually historical footnotes yet necessary to mention for the examination of older documents. These quick copies, all made from a master, can be divided into three basic techniques: spirit, stencil, offset.

Figure 8.1

A threatening note (a) received by the Netherlands Forensic Institute was compared to a reference copy (b) made by a suspect photocopier. Repeating indentation marks on both documents were traced back to have originated from the fusing roller (c) of the photocopier. Damage of the surface coating of this roller caused a toner build-up in these areas, hence resulting in impression marks in the paper of the produced photocopy. A close-up (d) of the identical impression marks on the fuser roller and the threatening note shows the similarities. (Research by: Jan A. de Koeijer, MSc. Photographed by: W.M.L. Huijben. Netherlands Forensic Institute, Volmerlaan 17, 2288 GD Rijswijk, The Netherlands)

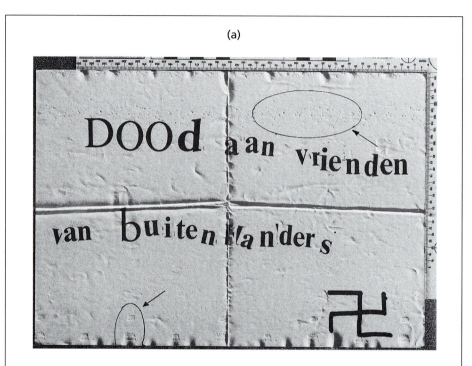

(a)

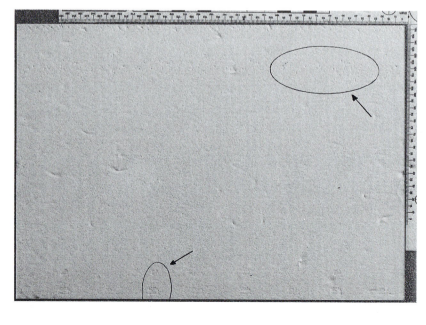

(b)

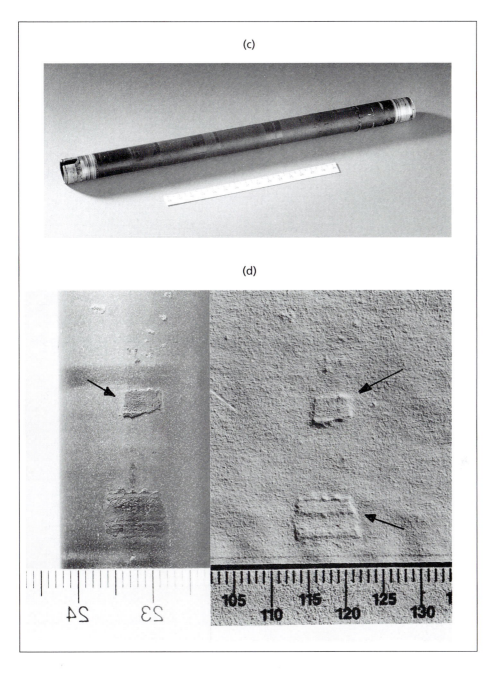

Figure 8.1
(continued)

In a spirit duplicator there can be either a direct impression or thermographic impression. In each case a specially treated sheet of paper is covered with a carbon sheet. The image is then transferred to the master, which is then mounted on the drum of the duplicator. Slightly moistened paper is fed through the duplicator, and an image is transferred.

Stencil or mimeograph copies are made by cutting a stencil. The image can be transferred from the stencil by direct impression, thermography, or electronic scanning.

Offset printers work very much like offset printing from plates, with transfer of the image by direct impression, electrostatic transfer, or pre-sensitized plates.

BIBLIOGRAPHY

Dick, Ronald M. (1979), "Duplicating Processes," Paper presented at the annual meeting of the American Society of Questioned Document Examiners, Rochester, New York.

NOTE

It cannot be stressed strongly enough that in document examination, documents produced on a copier do constitute material to be examined (though they can never be a substitute for the original should it be available).

It is certainly proper for an examiner just as anyone else, to use a photocopier, to copy documents for archival purposes. When the purpose of that archive is to record aspects of a questioned document for possible referral at a later date, regular photography is to be preferred.

A copy machine should never be used to produce illustrations for courtroom presentation. That is the function of standard photography.

SOURCES OF FURTHER INFORMATION

Xerox   http://www.xerox.com/factbook/1997/byr49-79.htm

CHAPTER 9

PHOTOGRAPHY

GENERAL

The role of document photography is to: (1) serve as an archival tool, recording material submitted for examination, (2) assist in viewing and recording facets of a document (e.g. IR, UV) not visible to the naked eye, and (3) aid in explaining conclusions. The purpose of this chapter is to highlight some of the photographic issues relevant to a document examiner, and not to serve as a basic photography text.

ARCHIVES

It is axiomatic in any forensic document laboratory that material submitted for examination be recorded for possible future use. Questioned documents are routinely returned to the authority submitting the material for examination. In the event that questions arise about the examination or there is a request for court testimony, some record should exist with the examiner.

The best method of recording is by photography, although some examiners use photocopies to cut down on costs.

Another method to avoid unnecessary expense without compromising quality is to photograph documents and develop the film to assure that it has been properly exposed, but not to make prints until they are needed. An alternative is to make contact prints for filing purposes.

EXAMINATION AND VISUALIZATION PHOTOGRAPHY

Numerous types of cameras are on the market today. In choosing one for document examination, one should remember the very steadfast rule that the film, the lens board, and the document to be photographed must be absolutely parallel to each other; if not, there can be distortions in the resultant photograph. The camera should, therefore, be one where this principle can be readily applied to documents. Therefore, hand-held cameras should not be used to photograph documents.

When using a camera, the best procedure is to place the document to be photographed under a sheet of glass on a flat surface beneath the camera with lens pointed downward. A small level is then placed on the glass covering the document and on the back of the camera. All pictures should have an inch or metric scale and show the case number of the document photographed. Color photographs should also contain a color scale.

There are numerous factors which affect a photograph – camera, lens, length of exposure, filters, photographic paper, etc. A log should be completed whenever a photograph is taken, so that specific answers can be given to questions about photographic conditions. For example, if an obliterated number is restored using IR film, a specific written record should be made of the type of film, filter, exposure time, etc.

Care should be taken that the proper lens of good quality is used. Certain cheaper products can distort photographs, and should not be used.

Selection of film is not an automatic procedure. In photographing documents, a full tone reproduction is what is desired. To photograph writing in pencil, for example, a film is needed with a heavier contrast than for pen writing: Wratten[1] filters 8 or 9 can be helpful. Photographing with IR and UV is discussed in Chapter 14.

Proper lighting is an important factor in photography. Oblique or side lighting (often at an angle of 2 to 5 degrees) can be an effective method of finding and recording writing or disturbed fibers in paper caused by an abrasive erasure. (Use of a blue filter such as C-5 can sometimes show color difference due to the use of a chemical eradicant; that same filter has also been used successfully to strengthen faded writing.)

[1] *These filters were named after Frederick Charles Luther Wratten (1840–1926) of Croydon, England. In 1878 he manufactured silver bromide gelatin plates, and in 1906 he manufactured panchromatic photographic plates.*

Figure 9.1

Note the fiber disturbance due to erasure. This case of a will in German included as writing exemplars a diary with notes covering the period 1950–1990 – all written with the same ball-point pen. (Courtesy of Lucia Marina, Cluj, Romania)

The use of inappropriate and/or improper methods and materials can distort photographs. In general police photography this can be profoundly significant when looking at the relative distance of two objects, the length of skid marks, the depth of a pit, etc. These same distortions can be found in photographs of documents; this can be seen in height and direction of lines, depth of impression, etc.

BIBLIOGRAPHY

Infrared and Ultraviolet Photography: Advanced Date Book M-3, Eastman Kodak Company, Rochester, New York. Updated periodically.

DEMONSTRATION

Although there are many benefits of showing an original document to a judge, enlargements also have a role to play. They can be much simpler to see, and they allow the document examiner to highlight detail that he feels is important. Side by side enlargements of more than one document can also be an effective way of demonstrating a comparison.

Slides using rear projection so as not to darken the room can be an effective tool in demonstration. The use of slides, however, should be restricted to matters of concept and demonstration, since they can be much less accurate than photograph prints. Instead of rear projection, which can be awkward to arrange in court, a viewer similar to a television can be used with the same effect. Some expert witnesses like to use a computer program similar to Power-Point®. This can be effective if used properly.

From the lawyer's perspective it should be remembered that the accuracy of a photograph can be challenged in court. This should be done when there is a question of distortion that is relevant to the case being tried.

ADVICE TO THE LAWYER

Documents can be important evidence in a case, and they can also change as time passes. This is specifically true in the case of burnt, water-soaked, or wrinkled documents. If the documents at hand are not to be given immediately to a document examiner for examination, they should at least be given to a document photographer for record filming.

BIBLIOGRAPHY

Scott, Charles C. (1969), *Photographic Evidence*, 3 vols, West Publishers, St Paul, Minnesota.

DIGITAL CAMERAS

At the time of writing there have been no court decisions causing basic problems as regards the use of digital cameras in forensic cases in general, or in document cases in particular.

MONTAGE

There have been cases of photo alteration – the most common instances being either the deletion or the addition of someone in a scene. With both procedures, extensive work must be done to the photograph. When something is deleted, new material must be added to fill the space. When something is added, the area on the photograph often must be "cleaned" to make room for the addition. Placing one picture on another is called "montage."

Photo montage can be detected by several methods: sloppy cleaning, contradictory shadows, contradictory camera angle, inconsistent printing nets.

Computers have substantially affected photo montage examinations. Today most montages are done through the computer manipulation of digitalized photographic images. The best way to detect these manipulations is through contradictory photographic angles. This is, of course, easier to discern in pictorial subjects than in written or printed texts.

BIBLIOGRAPHY

Langenbruch, H. (1935), "Zur Photomontagen Frage (On the Question of Photographic Montage)," *Vierteljahreszeitschrift für angewandte Kriminalistik*, 29: 29–34.

CHAPTER 10

WRITING INKS AND DYES, PENS AND PENCILS

WRITING INK

HISTORY

Ink has existed since it was used in the ancient world, for example in Ancient Egypt for writing on papyrus. These early inks used a carbonaceous compound base, and they can be divided into sepia inks (secretions from species of *cephalopoda* including *sepia officinalis*) and Indian/Chinese inks (carbonized organic substances). Such inks were in common use until approximately the twelfth century. Carbon inks are still in use today, but only for specialized purposes and not for general writing.

In the early twelfth century iron-gallotannate inks (nutgalls and tannin) became popular, although there is ample evidence that they were in use at a much earlier date. These inks combined with iron salts (ferrous sulphate) were blue or blue-green.

Over the centuries there have been numerous changes in ink formulation, for example the elimination of corrosion. Today inks for fountain pens tend to be either water based or glycol based. Vanadium (late nineteenth century) and aniline dye (invented 1861) inks are no longer in common use. In most fountain pens virtually any properly made writing ink can be used, even though many pen manufacturers try to promote sales of their own label ink.

As a point of curiosity, the original meaning of "blue-black" ink (invented in 1834 by Henry Stephens [England]) was not a description of a color, but rather of a process. The ink was blue (in the Stephens ink because of indigo) upon writing, but later after oxidation it turned black.

Characterization of early ball-point pen inks is clear. Until 1950, all inks had washable dyestuffs or iron gallotannate, and oil-based solvents. 1950 ushered in the era of glycol-based inks (ethylene glycol). Sometimes rosin or rosin acid was used to improve viscosity. Only in 1953, however, did ball-points become a popular item with the writing public. Copper phthalocyanine dyes (copper phthalocyanine tetrasulphonic acid) were introduced into inks experimentally in 1954 and commercially soon thereafter.

Some problems with the original ball-point inks were slow drying, broadening of written lines during the drying process, fading, and smudging.

Second generation ball-point inks are composed of a solvent (glycol or polyalcohol), a coloring agent, anti-corrosives, waterproofing, and "private" materials (which give commercial uniqueness to the product, such as anti-coagulants).

INK MANUFACTURE

In many ways the situation with ink and pens can be compared with that of typewriters. There are:

[1] *Examples are Formulabs, Chromex Mittenwald, National Ink, Chemie and Hartley.*

[2] *Examples are Bic, Parker, and Shaeffer.*

[3] *Examples are Anja and National Pen.*

- manufacturers of ink only[1],
- manufacturers of ink and pens[2],
- manufacturers of pens only[3]:
  - house label
  - outside label.

In most cases ink is purchased from a manufacturer, and the local "pen manufacturer" carries out the assembly and casting of the plastic pen housing.

INK DIFFERENTIATION

There have been numerous methods suggested to differentiate between two inks based on color. These are several of the more common methods:

1   *Light Examinations*, including:
   (a) Normal light (sunlight, and artificial: tungsten, halogen, fluorescent)
   (b) Filters in the visible range (397 nm–725 nm)
   (c) Infra-red (>725 nm) (IR)
   (d) Infra-red luminescence (IRL)
   (e) Ultra-violet (long wave [300–400 nm] and short wave [250 nm]) (UV).
   In many instances it is possible to view color differences under normal lighting conditions. When this is the case, photographs should be taken for record purposes. In the case, for example, of IR, often results can be obtained by viewing the document using an IR light source. In other cases special IR film will render better results.

2   *Thin layer chromatography (TLC)*. A sample of ink is removed from the paper, then it is placed in a tube and dissolved with a solvent. For ball-point inks common solvents are pyridine (unpleasant odor but quite effective), ethanol, butanol, acetone, ethyl acetate, amyl acetate (and others). A spot is then placed using a micro-pipet on a TLC or HPTLC plate (glass is to be preferred over aluminum despite higher cost), which is put into a tank to be developed. Several combinations of solvents can be used as eluents.

The same procedure is followed with the plain paper to eliminate confusion between paper and ink constituents.

When ink samples from two different documents are compared using TLC, one should preferably use the same TLC plate and the same batches of chemicals to exclude the possibility of outside influences on the examination results. This can be a useful issue for a lawyer to raise in court.

When the TLC patterns of two ink samples do not "match," this is usually sufficient basis to determine that the inks in question are different. When the TLC patterns *do* match, the results do not mean that the inks are necessarily the same. To go beyond a statement of "no differences were detected based upon testing conducted," further examination is necessary.

3   *Spectrophotometer.* For some inks the TLC plates are scanned on a spectrophotometer at 550-nm using xenon light.

4   *MECC.* Recently de Koeijer et al. (1997) have experimented with micellar electrokinetic capillar chromatography (MECC) to differentiate ink dyes. Encouraging results have been found with reducibility in the tests. Experiments have also been made using capillary electrophoresis (CE) and capillary zone electrophoresis (CZE).

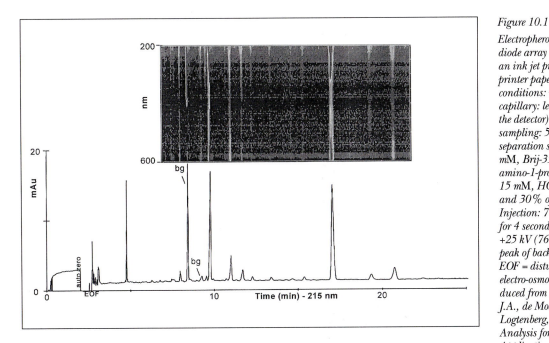

Figure 10.1

Electropherogram and photo-diode array contour map of an ink jet printer ink on printer paper. Experimental conditions: uncoated silica capillary: length 47 cm (40 to the detector)/50 µm i.d.; sampling: 5 dots of ink line; separation solution: SDS 60 mM, Brij-35 0.5 mM, 3-amino-1-propanol (pKa 10) 15 mM, HCl 7.5 mM, pH 10 and 30% of acetonitrile; Injection: 70 mbar (0.5 psi) for 4 seconds; electrophoresis: +25 kV (76 µA)/44°C. bg = peak of background (paper); EOF = disturbance caused by electro-osmotic flow. (Reproduced from Xu, X., de Koeijer, J.A., de Moel, J.J.M. and Logtenberg, H. (1997), "Ink Analysis for Forensic Science Applications by Micellar Electrokinetic Capillary Chromatography with Photo-diode Array Detection," International Journal of Forensic Document Examiners, 3(3) (July/September): 240–260)

It should be noted that the paper on which ink appears can have both a visual and chemical effect on the perceived color, thus caution should be taken when comparing ink colors with different papers serving as background. Therefore, one should always analysis the paper and "subtract" it from the ink as a control.

Determination of an ink formula can yield the earliest date that the ink was in use, hence the earliest date that the document could have been written. It is not possible to examine a document and determine from the ink when, after first ink manufacture, the document was prepared. For example, if the ink was first manufactured in 1930, it cannot be determined if the writing was made immediately thereafter or ten or twenty years later. Several modern methods claim to answer this question; however, at the time of writing definitive proof is lacking. It is sometimes possible to determine relative age of ink – if two writings on the same document were written at *roughly* the same period of time (in other words, if an alteration or addition was made to a document at a later time).

A common characteristic of many inks is fading, often as a result of oxidation. Although there are claims that particular methods can differentiate between "fresh" writing and "older" writing, these claims are made upon subjective methods most often related to iron gallate inks. There are no "fading standards" available, hence determination of age based upon fading should be regarded with professional skepticism.

The first modern "permanent" ink was invented by August Leonardi (Hannover, Germany) in 1856. This was based upon alizarin ($C_{14}H_8O_4$) and indigo ($C_{16}H_{10}N_2O_2$) (*indigofera*).

BIBLIOGRAPHY

Brunelle, Richard (1992), "Ink Dating: The State of the Art," *Journal of Forensic Sciences*, 37: 113–124.

Brunelle, Richard L. and Cantu, Antonio A. (1987), "A Critical Evaluation of Current Ink Dating," *Journal of Forensic Sciences*, 32(6) (November): 1522–1536.

Hilton, Ordway (1984), "Characteristics of Erasable Ball Point Pens," *Forensic Science International*, 26: 269-275.

Kelly, Jerry D. and Cantu, Antonio A. (1975), "Proposed Standard Methods for Ink Identification," *Journal of the Association of Official Analytical Chemists*, 58(1) (January): 122–125.

Sensi, Carl A. and Cantu, Antonio A. (1982), "Infrared Luminescence: Is it a Valid Method to Differentiate Among Inks?," *Journal of Forensic Sciences*, 27: 196–199.

Xu, X., de Koeijer, J.A., de Moel, J.J.M. and Logtenberg, H. (1997), "Ink Analysis for Forensic Science Applications by Micellar Electrokinetic Capillary Chromatography with Photo-Diode Array Detection: A Comprehensive Alternative Approach to Conventional Forensic Ink Analysis," *International Journal of Forensic Document Examination*, 3(3) (July-September): 240–260.

FOUNTAIN PENS

Ancient pens were made of reed (in China, also hairs). Only in the sixth century did the feather begin to be used widely for writing.

Traditional "pens" (often goose feather) were dipped into ink as the holder wrote. In 1809 Joseph Bramah (England) invented a machine to cut feather nibs according to several specifications, but the writing industry would soon move from the feather. Metal nibs, which would in a few decades entirely replace the feather quill, began to appear in 1780.

Thomas Sheldon opened the first factory for steel nibs in 1828. Two years later James Perry found a method to make steel nibs more flexible by adding slits, and he was followed a year later by William Joseph Gillott who again improved the nib by stamping it out from sheets of rolled metal.

In 1883 Lewis Edson Waterman (1837–1901) invented the first fountain pen (US Patent 293,545, issued 12 February 1884) which for the first time contained an ink reservoir inside the writing instrument with ink flowing by three fissures feed based upon capillary attraction. Previously attempted models of what is called the fountain pen had lacked an adequate system to regulate the flow of ink. The problem of corrosion from ink was solved in 1885 with the introduction of an ebonite storage tube which stayed an industry standard until the 1920s. Changes in temperature in pressure caused the ink to lose equilibrium and leak; this was corrected in 1910 with ladder-feed chambers which received excess ink[4].

At first refilling the pens was complicated and there were various methods in use, the most popular being the eyedropper; this was changed in 1908 by W.A. Shaeffer who invented the lifting lever principle of refilling (lever mechanism redesigned in 1912, US Patent 1,046,660). (Waterman introduced a self-filling pen in 1908 followed by its version of the lever filler in 1913.) In 1955 Parker (company founded in 1888 by George Parker [1863–1937]) introduced Model 61® (discontinued 1970) to prevent leakage when there is a difference of air pressure (such as in an airplane).

Many fountain pens today use cartridges for ink refill. In a cartridge pen (introduced by Shaeffer in 1954), the ink feed system begins to function when the nib touches the paper, and the ink moves through a capillary-like channel from the cartridge. In a well-made pen there is a storage area for extra ink left by excess pressure; the ink returns to the cartridge when pressure is lessened (when the writer lifts the pen). From an historical perspective the first step towards the cartridge was the Eagle pen which stored ink in a glass tube inserted into the holder; cartridges became practical only after the unbreakable plastic used in the disposable refills became inexpensive.

A major factor in determining the quality of writing is the nib of the fountain

4 *This can still be seen today particularly in certain fine point pens which can leak after change in air pressure (e.g. an airplane ride) when there is air in the ink chamber (i.e. when ink has been used and replaced by air).*

pen. The quality of the nib can determine shading in the writing; a steel nib (even when gold-plated) will not provide the flexibility found in a solid gold nib (often with an iridium tip). Likewise, if the inner radius of the nib is too large, ink will not flow evenly to the paper; if the radius is too small, there well might be scratching. Again, to improve writing, quality nibs are available specifically for left-handed and right-handed writers, as well as with different apertures to leave a different amount of ink (fine, medium, etc.) in the writing.

Typical Nib	Size (mm)
Extra fine	0.6
Fine	0.8
Medium	1.0
Broad	1.2
Extra broad	1.4

Other nibs are oblique/left angle (OF, OM, OB, OBB), steno (St), beginner's (A) and left-hand (L). The Montblanc Company, for example, sold more than 100 different types/sizes of nibs during the "Golden Age" of fountain pens in the 1930s. During that period an adjustable nib was also tried.

From the document examiner's perspective, a well-made fountain pen is an excellent tool, since it allows a skilled writer to exhibit mastery of the pen by shading of strokes. In many cases where a fountain pen has been used it is also possible to determine the direction of writing. It should be noted that many of the classic Questioned Documents texts were written in the age of the fountain pen; the illustrations in sections dealing with handwriting reflect the era. One should take into account the differences due to the writing instrument when quoting or reading from these texts.

In the 1930s there was a general redesign of pens to yield better balance, which was touted to improve the writer's penmanship. No respected source has claimed the ability to discern from a writing if it was done with a "balanced" pen.

Today, fountain pens account for a very small percentage of all pens sold. This is due both to cost and the problem of refilling, and to the relative ease of ballpoint usage. In developing countries and in parts of the Middle East, however, dip-writing instruments have been in extensive use even in the "modern" period.

BIBLIOGRAPHY

Lambrou, Andreas (1989), *Fountain Pens: Vintage and Modern*, Classic Pens Ltd, Epping, Essex, United Kingdom.

Lussato, Bruno (1992), "L'histoire du Stylo" (video), produced by OMAS, France.

COVERT INKS

Handwriting in "secret" or "covert" ink can be identified in just the same way as writing in regular ink. One of the primary problems in these examinations is that covert inks tend to be applied with soft writing implements so as not to leave visible indentations. The net result is line quality that does not show many of the characteristics normally present. With those inks that start out as invisible, since the writer does not see what he has written, there are sometimes differences of alignment, relative letter height, etc.

A major problem is to develop covert inks so they can be seen. The exact visualization process depends upon the formulation of the covert ink used. Two of the most common development methods for simple formulations are ultraviolet light and heating (caring not to burn the document). If the writing is not prepared properly, an ESDA® examination can yield results.

BIBLIOGRAPHY

Rubin, Samuel (1987), *The Secret Science of Covert Inks*, Loompanics Unlimited, Port Townsend, Washington.

BALL-POINT PENS

There is some controversy about the exact date of the first ball-point pen in trial runs in Europe in the 1930s. (Estimates run as high as 25,000 pens produced between 1935–1939, some by Biro and others by Klimes-Eisner.) The first commercial quantities, however, were produced by Laszlo and George Biro in Argentina in 1944. As the novelty of the pen decreased and more were manufactured, prices fell in New York from $12.50 when ball-points were first introduced in October 1945 by the Reynolds International Pen Company (which upstaged Eversharp who bought the Biro rights) to $0.25 three years later. In January, 1954 Parker was the first company to offer different sizes of ball-points.

The assembly of a ball-point pen has three essential parts: housing, ball, and ink in its container. The original balls were steel with a brass housing but now other materials are used, particularly for specialized situations such as writing on greasy surfaces.

From the perspective of the document examiner, aspects of writing are angle in which the pen is held, writing direction, and writing surface. These three aspects can influence the individual writing product. The housing of the pen will often determine how the pen is grasped, hence the writing angle. The ball will often leave a "path" or "track," aiding the examiner in determining the direction of writing. (An occasional trail of ink alongside the tract resulting from point wicking [dirt] can also be an indicator in determining writing direction.) Line width is more a function of the ball-point than it is of the writer.

BALL-POINT INK

Ball-point ink manufacture is a complicated process, which does not lend itself to small local factories. Major sources of inks are the United States, Germany, Japan and recently China.

How long does a ball-point pen last before the ink no longer functions? Obviously, there are numerous factors, including storage condition and weather. As a general guideline, ink stored in a plastic-type refill lasts for "several" years; ink housed in a metal refill should last for much longer. Blue inks also last longer than other colors.

Ball-point inks come in different colors that are made from numerous dyes. Blue ink, for example, is often composed of several different dyes and not just one pure "blue dye." This has numerous ramifications, including fading. For example, if an older writing is compared with a newer writing in the same ink and one of the dyes has faded faster than another, the composition of the ink might appear different, and the mistaken conclusion of two different inks could be reached.

Attempts have been made to date ball-pen inks by methods such as solvent extraction of dyes. The only reliable method to date the manufacture (*not* use) of these inks is by identifying constituents. In 1968 the United States Bureau of Alcohol, Tobacco and Firearms (ATF) took the initiative to develop an ink library, for ink identifications and dating. The library contains most American ball-point inks manufactured during the period 1958–1968, and all US ball-point inks manufactured since that time. No claim is made about the completeness of the non-US ink collection. The only known European collection of the 1960s, that of the Zurich Police, was incorporated into the ATF collection which was transferred to the United States Secret Service in 1988. Exemplars include both samples received from ink manufacturers (requested samples[5]) (including data on earliest date of manufacture) and pens/ink purchased in stationery stores (acquired samples[6]). This is done in cooperation with industry, and the system is predicated upon strict quality control and standardization in the manufacturing process. This project is by no means simple, since ink formulae can change quickly in response to market demands. The introduction, for example, of a new writing tip (e.g. extra fine or fine) can be reason for a new ink formula.

In 1975 ATF initiated the National Ink Tagging Program in which US ink factories periodically changed tags in their ink formulae, thus allowing period of manufacture dating. Tags were identified by using an analysis by x-ray fluorescence. Emphasis was placed on the dyes rather than on the vehicles.

[5] *Terminology of Tony Cantu, private correspondence.*

[6] *Ibid.*

In early 1979 an erasable ball-point blue ink was introduced to the market, first by Papermate, then by Scripto and Bic. It was erasable up to a week after writing using a soft eraser. At a later date black and red color options were also offered. Writing effected by these pens sometimes has small areas of non-inking, usually similar to potholes. Even after erasure (sometimes leaving luminescence in the area), indentation from the writing sometimes remains. Chemical treatment (erasure detection fluid) has also revealed the erased writing.

BIBLIOGRAPHY

Hilton, Ordway (1957), "Characteristics of the Ball Point Pen and Its Influence on Handwriting Identification," *Journal of Criminal Law, Criminology, and Police Science*, 47: 606–613.

FIBER (POROUS POINT) PENS

The Japanese company, Pentel, developed the first fiber-tip pen, in 1962. Mass marketing started the following year. The pen had a nylon-acrylic writing point.

These writing instruments generally hold ink in saturated form, such as on a piece of felt. A small capillary then brings the ink to the writing point that is usually a fiber. Felt tips, once the industry standard, have now been replaced with synthetics. Most common tips are: (1) felted materials such as polyester, polypropylene, (2) bonded fibers, and (3) porous plastic.

Fiber tip inks are primarily water-based with the addition of ethylene-glycol, diethylene glycol, and formamide; acid and base dyestuffs are also added. There are various formulations for the exact ink constituency. Erasable ink formulas for these and for rolling tip pens were introduced in the 1970s. Petroleum-based permanent inks (usually toluene or xylene solvents[7]) are also to be found.

A variation of the fiber tip is the plastic tip pen which has a hard plastic tip or encased porous tip. One reason for using these pens is that pressure can be applied to the writing paper, thus allowing copy paper (NCR/chemical or carbon) to be used.

These pens are non-refillable/disposable.

[7] *Benezene was previously used, but it was discontinued due to carcenogenic concerns. Toluene and xylene are now being replaced by higher alcohols such as amyl alcohol.*

BIBLIOGRAPHY

Zimmerman, Jeannine, Doherty, Paige and Mooney, Dennis (1988), "Erasable Felt Tip Writing Instrument Detection," *Journal of Forensic Sciences*, 33(3): 709–717.

ROLLER PENS

These pens, introduced in the early 1970s, use a rolling ball made from either metal or ceramic material. The water-based ink tends to leave a wider and more flowing line than is found in a traditional ball-point pen.

EXAMINATION CONCLUSIONS

Based upon chemical/physical analysis it can be possible to determine if the ink used in a document was available commercially on the date of the document.

Inks must be categorized as class evidence. That is to say, one cannot make the statement that two inks are "the same." Rather, one can only conclude that they belong to the same class. The document examiner can strengthen his conclusion only by showing the very limited size of a "class" in terms of pens manufactured.

BIBLIOGRAPHY

Cantu, Antonio A. (1995), "A Sketch of Analytical Methods for Document Dating: Part I0. Static Approach: Determining Age Independent Analytical Profiles," *International Journal of Forensic Document Examiners*, 1(1): 40–51.

Crown, David A., Brunelle, Richard L. and Cantu, Antonio A. (1976), "The Parameters of Ballpen Ink Examinations," *Journal of Forensic Sciences*, 21: 917–922.

Miller, Fred M. (1951), "The Age of Ink," *Proceedings of the American Academy of Forensic Sciences*, 1(1): 138–154.

PENCILS

Penciled writing presents a document examiner with a much different situation than ink, since the quality of the writing can be somewhat different. From the perspective of identification of the writer, it can be totally possible to reach a definitive conclusion based upon the examination of a text written in pencil.

It is not possible to date writing based upon the pencil, nor is it generally possible to determine if two writings were done with the same pencil. In general terms the writing element in most pencils is a combination of graphite (softer) and clay (harder), and the ratio determines hardness[8] ("harder" pencils leave less material on the writing surface). With this said, it is extremely difficult to analyze the graphite/clay to determine differences between two pencils and all the more so between two penciled writings.

Common parlance mentions the "lead" pencil, however that is a basic mistake. In 1564 a large supply of an extremely pure material thought to be "lead" was discovered in Borrowdale, Cumberland (England). The material was very effective in writing, and only in 1779 was it determined to be a form of

[8] *A binder and waxes are also present.*

carbon. Ten years later Abraham Werner gave it the name, "graphite[9]," from the Greek root meaning to write or to draw. This graphite became the basic material in the "pencil," a word that entered English in the fourteenth century when it meant a drawing brush (from Latin). In this early period chunks of Borrowdale graphite were wrapped in string to keep the hands of the writer clean, and the string was removed as it became necessary to uncover more of the graphite. Experiments were made constantly, and in 1761 Kaspar Farber started in Nurnburg, Germany, what has become the world's oldest pencil company still operating.

Pencils similar to those in use today started in 1795 when Nicolas Jacques Conte (1755–1805)[10] (France) mixed graphite with water and clay (rather than sulfur), pressed the material into a wooden holder, then baked the mixture at extremely high temperature. (Some give the credit to Hardtmuth of Vienna, Austria, who worked at about the same time.) Original pencil manufacture was primarily in Germany; in 1812 William Monroe made the first pencils in the United States. Joseph Priestly (England) invented the first "vegetable gum eraser" in 1770, and Hyman Lipman (Philadelphia) patented the first pencil with an eraser affixed atop in 1858.

In the nineteenth century pencils using slate instead of graphite were manufactured; however, these were unsuccessful and were discontinued.

Today pencils are made from graphite powder, clay and water. The ratio of graphite to clay determines the hardness of the pencil. There is, however, variation in raw materials and manufacturing standards since no exacting international standards of hardness exist in the pencil industry. Thus, a 4H pencil of one company might very much resemble 3H (or 5H) of another company. The only international supervision of pencils is health testing of the lacquer covering the housing. This is done by international agreement for the protection of children who often chew the pencil housing; maximum limits are set for Pb, Hg, Ba, Sb, Cd, Se, As and Cr.

The amount of graphite laid down on a page during the courses of writing is due to the hardness of the graphite in combination with the quality/characteristics of the raw materials. The graphite stays on the surface of the paper and does not penetrate as ink does. Writing with harder pencils often leaves a pressure groove in the paper, however the writing is still on the surface (albeit indented or "lowered").

[9] The same route also gives the word "graffito" and more known plural "graffiti," which are first recorded in English in the nineteenth century, graph, and graphic.

[10] The modern Conte brand pencil was named after this person. The manufacturer is BIC.

Pencil Symbol	Hardness
H	hard
B	black (soft)
HB	half black (medium)
F	fine

This chart can also be expressed in more detail by the following (not all pencil companies make all types; others make types to the right or left of this chart):

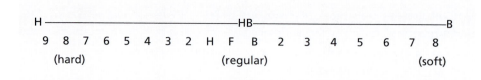

One large international pencil manufacturer based in Europe regards "regular" pencils for ordinary use as 3B to F. Another sources describes "regular" pencils as 3B to 3H.

There is no standard for the diameter of a pencil. In addition to specialized and professional pencils, wide diameters and thick casings are often given to children first learning to write. The thicker pencil is more appropriate to their hand/finger motor development.

Jacobson (Germany) first made colored pencils in 1874; he used aniline ($C_6H_5NH_2$) instead of graphite. Today numerous pigments are used in colored pencils. The composition of the colored pencil is colorant, filler, lubricant (wax-like material) and a binder (usually methyl cellulose or polyvinyl alcohol). There are also colored pencils made for numerous specialized purposes in addition to writing, such as drawing and draftsmanship. The pencils also come in differing quality (hence the different selling prices in the marketplace).

From an historical perspective, John Isaac Hawkins invented the mechanical pencils in 1822 and soon thereafter sold the manufacturing rights to Sampson Mordan. The first practical mechanical pencil with a turning point was invented in 1912 by Tokuji Hayakawa; it was popular and began to be marketed in the United States two years later under the Ever-Sharp label. In these pencils the lead is inserted manually (either single lead or several pieces) into a multiple lead holder. There is no proven method to determine if writing has been done using a regular or a mechanical pencil.

There are also pencils with a plastic (rather than wooden) housing that have been introduced into the market. This, of course, has no direct influence on the written product. One company that makes these pencils (only HB) uses synthetic resins as well as graphite in the writing element.

PAPER

HISTORY

The history of paper goes back many centuries. In ancient times the "paper" used was parchment made from animal skins and papyrus, a cross-woven series of reeds pressed into a thin layer. Paper as we know it was invented by Ts'ai Lun, a Chinese man who lived some two thousand years ago. His "recipe" was simple: (a) he combined mulberry bark, hemp, and rags with water; (b) then he made a pulp (c) which was squeezed into thin sheets (d) to remove excess water, and (e) hung to dry.

As papermaking spread from the Orient to the Middle East and to Europe, the process remained slow and costly until 1798. In that year Nicholas Louis Robert (1761–1828), working in a papermill in Essenay, France, revolutionized the industry by inventing a mechanized procedure to replace manual labor. His new invention could produce paper in continuous long rolls rather than in single sheets. The Fourdrinier brothers, Henry and Sealy, bought the invention, but economic success was precluded by the high cost of rags that were needed for the pulp and the need to dry the papers produced. This problem was solved by the invention of drying cylinders by Thomas Bonsor Crompton (England) in 1820.

In the mid-nineteenth century other developments pushed papermaking closer to the modern era. Ground-wood paper was first made on a commercial basis in Saxony in 1847. In 1850 Friedrich Gottlob Keller developed a machine to grind wood into fibers, and in 1857 Thomas Routeledge introduced esparto paper. A very significant discovery was made in 1865 when C.B. Tilghman invented a sulfite procedure to dissolve wood resins. With these developments paper became an inexpensive commodity and the foundation for a new era in written communications. The first "modern" paper factory opened in Curtisville, Massachusetts, in 1867.

MANUFACTURE

An overall look at the paper industry today will show that only about half of the wood fibers used in paper are from trees cut for the purpose. In the late 1980s about 22% of the fibers in paper were from recycled waste paper, and approximately 23% came from the waste and residue of lumber operations. The clear trend in the paper industry is to move toward greater use of fibers from recycled paper products, thus minimizing the need for virgin fibers from newly cut trees. From a Questioned Documents perspective, this means that it will be increasingly difficult to source paper based on the geographic area in which trees (fibers) are grown. (Increased trade of raw products has already made this approach very difficult.)

In many countries it is not at all economical, practical or ecologically possible to cut trees for papermaking. The main sources of wood fiber are, therefore, imports from abroad (dried pulp in large, thick sheets) and recycled paper.

It should be pointed out that although recycling is considered a positive act from an environmental perspective, it has certain drawbacks: (a) pulp from recycled paper can be no better than the original product (almost always a mixture of qualities), and (b) fibers cannot be re-used indefinitely, since they break down.

Much of our modern paper is made from the small cellulose fibers found in wood. These are held together by lignin. When the sap, resin and lignin have been removed from these fibers by chemical means, the resultant fibers are called chemical pulp. When the wood is ground into minute pieces, the result is ground-wood pulp.

In simplified terms, the pulp is cooked in large digesters. Then it is blown under pressure to separate the fibers and remove extraneous materials. Next, it is bleached if necessary, then it is put into a beater where color and size (water resistance) can be added. After the beater the pulp is then sent to refiners where the fibers are cut to standard size. The pulp, still 99% water, is then sent to a Fourdrinier wire where excess water is removed. Finally the paper is dried and calendered (application of a finish, if desired).

When color is added to the pulp it is done with dyes. These can be divided into several types: (a) acid, (b) basic, (c) direct (d) other (sulfur dyes, organic and natural pigments). Although obvious color differences can be discerned by the naked eye, in other instances it is necessary to use chemical analysis, spot tests and chromatography to differentiate colors. It should be remembered that even white paper can have dyes (fluorescent brighteners, etc.). Other chemicals can also be added to the pulp for a variety of reasons. The following table lists some of the many chemicals that are commonly used.

Chemical	Purpose
Starches	Strength
Kaolin	Coating, filling
Alum	Sizing, Ph control
Waxes	Sizing, coating
Polyethylene resin	Extrusion coating
Rosin	Sizing
Calcium carbonate	Coating, filling

Fillers were first used as adulterants in paper, since a substance such as clay is clearly cheaper to use than wood fibers, but it was soon discovered that these fillers provide a sheet of paper which is more suitable for printing. Commonly used fillers are: kaolin (clay), calcium carbonate, calcium sulfate, barium sulfate, talc, titanium dioxide, zinc sulfide, and silica. The basic method to determine whether fillers are present in a sheet of paper is x-ray diffraction (XRD).

Watermarks, such as those in the currency notes of an increasing number of countries, are familiar to all of us. There are several important dates in the history of watermarks:

105	Invention of watermark (China)
1280	First use of a wire watermark (or 1282)
1690	William Rittenhouse makes the first American paper with watermark
1800	Johannot Mill (France) makes first multi-level/shaded watermark
1826	First wooden dandy roll
1839	William Joyson receives dandy roll patent
1959	"Customark" chemical watermark introduced

The principle of traditional watermarks is very simple. While the pulp is still wet, fibers can be moved. In places with fewer fibers, more light will pass through the paper; in places with more fibers, less light will pass. The watermark is the resultant effect. The most common method to make a watermark is to pass the wet pulp between a roller and another hard surface (often another roller) where the roller is equipped with a dandy roll. This is a wire mesh with a slightly raised picture or legend. The height of the picture or legend will determine how much fiber is pushed away as the pulp is passed, thus creating the mark.

In many security documents there are shadow or multi-tone watermarks, adding complexity to the forger's efforts to produce an imitation.

In the embossed method the paper is pressed between steel rollers when the paper is almost dry. This method is commonly used to place watermarks on certificates.

In 1959 an American company introduced Customark®, a chemical watermark allowing greater resolution than is found in dandy roll marks. Customark can be used only on white or off-white sheets; with other colors the "watermark" appears to be wet. The basic sales point of Customark is that for small production quantities it is cheaper than a genuine watermark.

Watermarks are particularly important in document examination cases since they can provide security and a means of dating. If, for example, a particular watermark was introduced in a given year, documents dated before then are forgeries. This dating can be overt, coded or totally discreet. One help in dating is that there are very few dandy roll manufacturers in the world (only five or six in the United States), hence checking records is not an impossible task. Paper manufacturers themselves are usually quite cooperative in assisting. There are, in fact, numerous paper manufacturers who intentionally introduce minor differences into their watermarks at periodic intervals to assist in dating.

The final step in the paper manufacturing process is for the paper to be cut from long rolls into sheets; 24 or 25 sheets (more common) are a squire, and there are 20 squires to a ream (today 500 sheets). The most common paper sizes conform either to the American measurements or the European DIN standards. Although European countries most often use DIN, American paper (such as 8.5″ × 11″ letter size[1]) is common for uses such as computer printers.

Paper is also "sized." That is to say that glutinous or gelatinous materials are added to fill spaces between fibers. Historically, this sizing was from either animal or vegetable products. Today most sizing is artificial or vegetable (often tree resins). "TS" indicates tub-sized paper (better quality), and "ES" means engine-sized (poorer quality). When writing on a paper that has not been sized (such as blotting paper), ink will spread and feather. Very often eradicating fluid will remove the sizing, thus complicating writing again in the same area.

[1] Sometimes the European cuts of American paper sizes are slightly off-size, since they are made according to metric approximations of inch measurements.

BIBLIOGRAPHY

Browning, B.L. (1977), *Analysis of Paper*, 2nd edn. Marcel Dekker, New York.

Caywood, Douglas (1995), "Watermarks and the Questioned Document Examiner," *International Journal of Forensic Document Examiners*, 1(4): 299–304.

Graff, J.H. (1940), *A Color Atlas for Fiber Identification.* Institute of Paper Chemistry, Appleton, Wisconsin.

Grant, Julius (1961), *A Laboratory Handbook of Pulp and Paper Manufacture.* Edward Arnold, London.

Hunter, Dard (1943), *Papermaking: The History and Techniques of an Ancient Craft.* Knopf, New York.

Lockwood's Directory of Paper and Allied Trades. Lockwood Publishing Company, New York. Published annually.

Phillip's Paper Trade Directory of the World. S.A. Phillips & Company, London. Published annually.

Studney, John (1951), "Characteristics and Uses of Writing Papers," Paper presented at Conference for World Defense and Internal Security, Philadelphia.

Toker, Bernard (1983), *Dictionary of Pulp and Paper: English–Hebrew,* Zohar Publishing, Jerusalem.

SPECIALTY PAPERS

Over many decades there have been numerous attempts to develop safety or security paper that will be difficult to imitate and will show all types of alterations. Imitation is generally made difficult by the use of special papers containing:

- Watermarks – custom made for the requester; maximum security obtained with the use of complex three-dimensional shaded watermarks.
- Planchettes – colored dots imbedded into paper in the manufacturing process.
- Fibers – colored or fluorescent fibers placed in the paper during the manufacturing process.
- Security threads – usually a polyester strip embedded into paper during the manufacturing process; these threads can be designed for visual inspection or machine readability.

High quality printing, often involving skilled engraving and printing, is another guard against unauthorized duplication. Alterations are prevented using special printing inks and background tints.

Carbon paper is a specially made sheet usually coated with an ink made of wax, oil, dyes and pigments. Different formulations have been developed to support various types of use. In offices abroad that still use carbon paper, single-use carbon sheets fastened to paper are quite common.

No carbon required (NCR) paper was introduced by the National Cash Register Company in 1954. With NCR paper, the user writes on the top sheet, and the image is transferred to lower sheets without the use of carbon paper. The transfer is accomplished through microencapsulated chemicals that are released from the pressure of writing. Over the years there have been changes in the chemical formula in NCR paper, and on that basis dating can be established.

BIBLIOGRAPHY

Bouffard, Philip (n.d.), "The Dating of NCR Paper," unpublished paper.

Purtell, David J. (1965), "Carbon Papers and Carbon Copy Impressions," Paper presented at the annual meeting of the American Society of Questioned Document Examiners, Ottawa, Ontario.

Simons, Francis L. (1951), "Safety Papers: A review of theory and practice," *Technical Association of the Pulp and Paper Industry*, 34 (10): 113A–122A.

EXAMINATION

Paper examination is a very specialized subject; however there are several questions that are frequently asked of document examiners.

CLASSIFYING

Sometimes it is necessary to know the type of paper. Such matters as the specific type of printing paper or the strength of wrapping paper are best referred to an industry specialist unless the document examiner has a uniquely strong background.

COMPARING

When asked if two pieces of paper are from the same sheet, the document examiner must first determine if the class characteristics in each piece are consistent. This would include weight and apparent color, then fiber and filler analysis. Assuming that there are no contradictions of class, individual features such as tear marks should be examined. For this purpose a high magnification is needed, either from a high powered microscope or from a scanning electron microscope (SEM). Unless there are tear marks, the examination rarely yields more than a statement of the presence/absence of similar characteristics.

It is sometimes possible to determine if two sheets of paper are from the same source (manufacturing plant or batch run) based on paper content. It is critical to remember that this is class evidence, and it should be remembered that hundreds of thousands of sheets might fit that very same description.

FIBER IDENTIFICATION AND CLASSIFICATION

It is sometimes necessary to identify from which fibers a particular piece of paper was made. This can be done with a number of iodine stains, the most

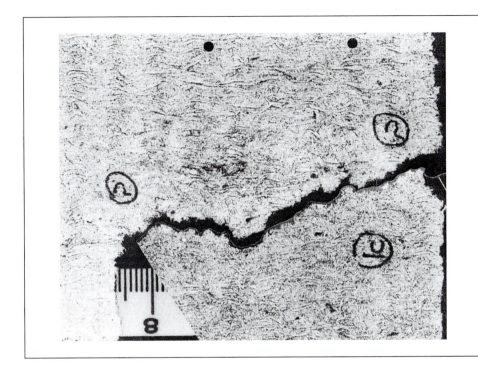

Figure 11.1
Two sheets of paper are compared along the tear. For convenience the originals were photographed, and the photographs were prepared. There are numerous similarities but there are also differences, suggesting that several pages might have been torn at the same time. (Courtesy of the Israel Police)

popular of which are Graff "C" stain or Herzberg Solution. With the use of iodine stains, the following colors appear:

- ground-wood – yellow
- chemical wood – blue
- rag – red/purple

(These are rough approximations. There are variations according to the exact iodine based solution used and its specific preparation.) Using a fiber atlas as a reference tool, it is possible to examine fibers under a microscope and determine from which type of trees they came.

DATING

As mentioned above, watermarks can be important in dating. There are, however, certain key dates in the history of papermaking which can also be important in this respect. Modern examples of these dates are:

1953 Introduction of organic synthetic fibers

c. 1940 Luminescent pigments

c. 1950 Optical whiteners

Other key dates for the introduction of new processes and materials are available in professional literature.

The commercial product, Post-It® (a slip of paper with a light adhesive to allow sticking and easy removal from paper stock), was introduced in 1974.

AUTHENTICITY

In many security documents the paper is made under strict controls and according to a standard formula. Deviation from the known formula can be grounds for a conclusion of non-authenticity. If, for example, a United States passport is made without a watermark, that alone is sufficient grounds for a determination of non-authenticity.

Watermarks are difficult to counterfeit but that is not to say that people have not tried. The primary method is to print a watermark on a page. Alternatively, some forgers have resorted to drawing the mark with an oil-based substance. Another method is to produce a cachet with the desired watermark design, then "stamp" the cachet on the page with correction fluid thinner rather than ink. Only a major operation can think of trying to manufacture paper with a "genuine" watermark.

One examination of watermarks, which can provide effective results, is ultra-violet light. A genuine watermark will react no differently from the sheet of paper when viewed under UV. Chemical watermarks, however, can often be detected with a UV light source. Since some chemical marking processes are more sensitive to long wave than to short wave, both should be used.

A definitive method of authenticating a watermark is through x-ray photography. Recording a watermark is done by photography using transmitted light.

A general word about watermark examinations. Watermarks can be a shortcut to the paper manufacturer from whom additional technical details might be obtained. Many American watermarks can be traced in Lockwood's Directory; Phillip's is useful for European manufacturers. In using these directories it should be remembered that there might be many companies using a watermark saying something common, such as "Extra Strong Bond." Thus, it can be important to photograph the questioned watermark and compare it point-by-point with knowns before a source is determined.

There are numerous other security features in various papers. It is necessary to examine each type of document knowing which security features it should have.

BIBLIOGRAPHY

Clement, J.L., Tiffes, D. and Ceccaldi, P.F. (1980), "Counterfeit Watermarks on False French Identity Documents," *International Criminal Police Review (Interpol)*, no. 334 (January): 2–7.

BIBLIOGRAPHY – GENERAL

Brunelle, Richard L. and Reed, Robert W. (1984), *Forensic Examination of Ink and Paper*, Charles C. Thomas, Springfield, Illinois.

Grant, Julius (1973), "The Role of Paper in Questioned Document Work," *Journal of the Forensic Science Society*, 13: 91–95.

Institute of Paper Chemistry (1979), *Forensic Paper Examination and Analysis*, Bibliographic Series 286, Institute of Paper Chemistry, Appleton, Wisconsin.

TEARS

A common examination is to determine if two torn pieces of paper came from the same sheet. This is determined by matching the tear design and by showing fibers on one side of the tear line that continue on the other side. If the tear pattern matches but fibers are not shown, one should consider the possibility that the fragments in question originated from several sheets torn at the same time.

There is no way to determine the numeric probability that two fragments were once one sheet of paper, since such factors as fibers, stains, and tear patterns cannot be quantified.

BIBLIOGRAPHY

Nichols, L.C. (1956), *The Scientific Examination of Crime*, Butterworth & Company, London, p. 302.

BURNT PAPERS

Often it is necessary to decipher writing on burnt pieces of paper. There have been numerous methods suggested and tried: ashing (Mitchel), chloralkydrate solution (Walls and Taylor), silver nitrate (Murray). These are basically of historical interest only. The basic method in use today is IR.

CHAPTER 12

ERASURES, OBLITERATIONS AND ALTERATIONS

ERASURES

An erasure can be either mechanical or chemical. In a *mechanical* erasure such as with the traditional "rubber" eraser, an abrasive movement is made upon the writing to be erased. In many cases of standard writing materials, abrasion of the paper can be seen either with a microscope or side light. As a general rule, the better the paper, the less visual sign of erasure, particularly when the action is done gently. (Microscopic examination can often show signs of fiber movement and traces of the erasing "rubber.")

Indicators of a mechanical erasure can be fiber disturbance often resulting in paper roughness, or smudging of writing.

In a *chemical* erasure, a solution is placed on the writing. This will not be effective if the ink is permanent. In any case, evidence of the use of a chemical erasing compound can frequently be found by viewing the document in UV (both long and short wave); metallic salts have the tendency to retain the erasing solution at a UV wavelength. Common substances to effect a chemical erasure are hypochlorites, dilute acids (hydrochloric, citric, oxalic), potassium permanganate, sodium hydrosulfite. In many cases these substances remove the ink dye or color agent, but they leave chemical reactions, if not the entire original writing, in the fibers; the object of an examination is to restore those reactions to visibility, i.e. to read the obliterated writing.

Indicators of a chemical erasure can be reaction when viewed with special lights and/or with filters, or when treated chemically.

In general, pencil writing cannot be erased chemically due to the ability of graphite to withstand most chemicals.

There has been some success in viewing erased text by use of an argon-ion laser (introduced into use in 1977). Best results have been at 488 nm and 514.5 nm using Wratten filters 15 and 22.

Another procedure used for "erasure" is an obliteration – not to erase a text, but to cover it with a pasted text or to cut it out and paste in the hole (to maintain uniform paper thickness).

As is true in most examinations, even the best technical equipment cannot replace a careful visual examination by a trained document examiner.

Sometimes erasures are made to allow a new text to be written. At other times the purpose of an erasure is simply to remove text.

In the 1970s and 1980s numerous companies marketed an erasable typewriter which allowed a typist to make corrections with relative ease. This was based upon a white ribbon designed to cover up printing from the black ribbon.

BIBLIOGRAPHY – ERASURES

Hilton, Ordway (1991), *Detecting and Deciphering Erased Pencil Writing*, Charles C. Thomas, Springfield, Illinois.

OBLITERATION
COMPUTER IMAGING

In recent years there have been numerous attempts to restore obliterated writing through computer imaging. The basic technique is that by using a scanner and appropriate software, layers of writing can be removed. These techniques are open to arguments of subjective erasure of writing. While the methods certainly have an examination value of raising possibilities to the examiner, at this point they are not sufficiently developed to allow for uncontested introduction into court evidence, since they raise the possibility of altering evidence.

CORRECTING RIBBON

Typewriter correcting ribbons (stored on the typewriter, such as on the "Correcting Selectric") do not erase mistaken typewriting. They merely cover the mistakes with a white impression that is supposed to blend into the sheet of paper. Again, concentrated light illumination from beneath the document is generally sufficient to read the document.

CORRECTING TAPE

In the 1960s correcting tape was popular for typewriters. This was a chalk on a paper (special paper was manufactured for carbon copy correction) which was placed over the mistaken letter. The incorrect letter was typed, the paper was removed, then the correct letter was typed. In the mid-1990s an advanced lay-down covering tape was introduced into the market.

CORRECTION FLUID

This is used for both typed/printed text and handwriting. In this system liquids were introduced to "paint" over the letters. This generally included a white paint in one bottle and trichloroethane, a dilutant, stored in a second bottle. The latter was prohibited by the Montreal Agreement since it served as a sniffing material, creating the need for a "one bottle" system. In most cases it is sufficient to shine a concentrated light through the document to read the original text, though at times it is necessary to use IR (illuminated from under the document). Alternative methods suggested have been cracking of the fluid through freezing, and the use of freon. In this regard, words of warning are in order. Although physically removing correcting fluid might sound simple, the legal ramifications of proving the non-existence of an intermediate layer should be taken into consideration. The same can be said regarding chemical removal of stains intended to obliterate writing.

Correction fluid has been manufactured in numerous countries; although most often white, in many countries it does come in a number of different colors to match the paper used (reported in blue, gray, green, off-white/ivory, pink, yellow, and shades thereof).

OTHER ALTERATIONS

In addition to erasures and obliterations, alterations also include additions/insertions to documents. These can be identified as follows:

- Typewritten – differences in font, fabric strands in cloth ribbon, ribbon type or chemical/color composition; irregularity in vertical or horizontal alignment.
- Printed– different method of printing, different font, different ink composition.
- Handwritten – differences in handwriting style, different ink composition.

Examples of documents frequently altered by adding materials are checks (raising the amount) and wills (adding conditions, terms, and beneficiaries). (In the case of wills, care should be taken to ascertain that the date has not been altered, since in most countries the latest dated will is the one legally binding.)

There are also page additions to assembled documents. This can be something as "simple" as removing a staple, inserting or changing a page, then reassembling the document. (In this case the staple should be inspected for signs of bending or manual closure, or in the case of a new staple conformity to other staples used by the source. The staple holes should also be examined for irregularities, unexplained tears and extra holes. There have been "ballistics-type" examinations of toolmarks left by staplers on the staples; however these examinations are much more a curiosity than an established routine.)

Passports are an example of a formally bound document which is sometimes disassembled, pages deleted or inserted, then the document resewn. For examination guidelines, see the section on passports.

Figure 12.1

In this lottery ticket three identical numbers constitute a winning card. In the lower card (b) the owner appears to have won 400 Shekels. The upper card (a), photographed in infra-red, reveals how "100" was altered to "400."
(Courtesy of Israel Police)

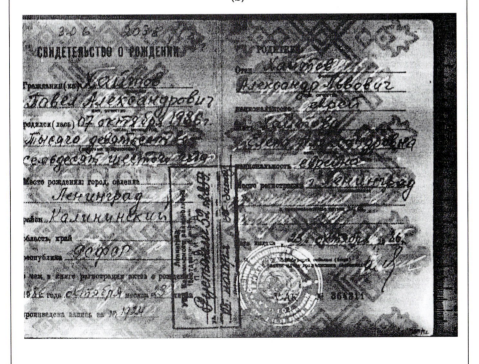

Figure 12.2
USSR birth certificate.
Alterations can be seen in
infra-red in the lower
picture (b).

CHAPTER 13

OFFICE SUPPLIES

PAPER CLIPS

Paper clips, or bent pieces of metal used to fasten pages, have been used since the middle of the nineteenth century. In the United States the first patent on a paper clip was issued to J.A. Harvey in 1856. Previous to that time documents had been fastened by cloth strings, often made of linen, silk, or cotton.

In 1835 John Ireland Howe had invented a machine for the rapid production of pins. This machine was adapted to fasteners, and commercial production began.

Over the years there have been a number of styles in clips. The standard paper clips today are gem and collette. Clips with a semi-pointed end (instead of round) are known as gothic. Ideal style clips are common for fastening larger groups of paper.

For older documents the date of introduction of clips can be important in authentication of age. The impression or indentation left by a clip can also be an indication that a clip had been in place; it is not possible to determine how long a clip was in place. Examination of an indentation should also include a close look for metal and rust marks as another indication that a clip had been used.

BIBLIOGRAPHY

Morris, Danny A. and Morris, Ronald N. (1973), "Paper Fasteners and Clips," Paper presented at the annual meeting of the American Society of Questioned Document Examiners, Silver Spring, Maryland.

STAPLES

Whenever small holes appear in a questioned document, the possibility of staples should be examined. The first step to take is to measure the distance between the holes to determine if the holes meet the class characteristics of staples.

There have been cases where examination was made to determine if two staples were emplaced from the same stapler. The technique is to compare the toolmarks on the staples when viewed under heavy magnification. (Criminalists or ballistics workers can also conduct this examination.)

ADHESIVE TAPE

HISTORY

Masking tape was introduced in 1925 in response to a need in the automotive industry to provide straight lines when spray painting[1]; this tape, based upon a paper strip and a glue, was laid down, the area spray painted, then the tape was removed. Although "Scotch®" tape is an Americanism for "cellophane tape," masking tape was, in fact, the first product to bear this name. This "Scotch Masking Tape" was the precursor of the "Cellophane[2]" or "Transparent Tape" invented by Richard G. Drew in 1930 based on the development of cellophane by Jacques Edwin Brandenberger in 1908. Contrary to its appearance as a simple product, the manufacture of cellophane tape is a complicated process, which limits the number of factories producing a successful product.

ADHESIVES

These tapes have two basic components: the adhesive and the "tape." The adhesives can be further divided into three types: acrylic, solvent and hot melt.

- *Acrylic.* A Swiss company is the predominant international supplier of acrylic adhesives to tape manufacturers.
- *Solvent.* These adhesives are produced by many companies. They are rubber-based.
- *Hot melt.* These adhesives are also widely produced, and they are based upon petroleum by-products, resin, and other additives. The exact components and their relative proportions change, hence it is often possible to determine if two pieces of tape with adhesive came from the same production batch.

Acrylics are the only glues that can be absolutely transparent. Hot melt will always have a trace of color.

TAPES

Tapes are made from different types of *material.* Masking tapes are made from paper or cloth. The "plastic" tapes are made from PVC (using only solvent adhesives) or polypropylene (using all three types of adhesive). Colored tapes can get their "color" either from the tape or from the adhesive. In fact, the vast

[1] Automatic paint spray guns had been recently invented.

[2] Although "cellophane tape" started out as the commercial name of a product, today it is a generic name for transparent tape. "Scotch" tape is still a registered trademark but in colloquial speech it is also often used as a generic descriptor.

majority of these tapes are transparent and receive the color from the adhesive.

As tape is removed from the roll, it is necessary to insure that the tape is removed smoothly. PVC/acrylic tapes are thermally treated to allow *release*. Hot melt tapes contain a release agent, usually in the quantity of approximately 4 grams per square meter of tape. (The tape is, in fact, also unwound in the manufacturing process. Standard procedure is to apply adhesive to rolls of 6.143 m^2. The rolls are then unwound to the length of tape required on a spool, the long roll is cut into numerous small spools, and then the process is started again.)

In a quality product there is more than one type of glue to allow the tape to hold and not peel or crack in different climates. There reportedly are some large exporters which manufacture different glue types for the climatic conditions of export clients.

Tape is often made in long rolls that are *cut* to produce smaller rolls of various widths. Thus, it is entirely possible that tapes of different widths will have exactly the same chemical constituents. Cutting of the tape is done either by pressure (leaving a mat or rough side) or razor (leaving a smooth or shiny side). Razor cutting is done when the exact width of the tape on the spool is critical.

Transparent tape comes in different *thickness*. PVC is standard at 32 µm to 35 µm; special order is up to 50 µm. Polypropylene tape is not as consistent. In the Far East the general standard is usually 22 gr/m^2 (tolerance of ± 0.5 gr), in Southern Europe 28–30 gr, and in the United States, Germany and Switzerland 35 gr.

Pliability is another factor in tapes. There is non-directional (rigid, stiff), mono-directional and bi-directional ply. Tape used as a handle on a package is often mono-directional. Cellophane tape in an office is usually bi-directional.

There are tape manufacturing companies which manufacture under a series of commercial names (often written inside the spool), including supply under contract for other tape manufacturing companies.

Printing is usually done on PVC tapes.

EXAMINATIONS

It is difficult to associate a commonly produced tape with a specific manufacturer. It is possible, however, to determine if two pieces of tape can be traced to a common source or manufacturing batch. A photospectrometer is a key piece of equipment in these examinations.

CHAPTER 14

FINGERPRINTS ON DOCUMENTS

INTRODUCTION

In many cases there is a chance that the fingerprints of the guilty person might be found on a document to which he had no explicable legal access. In a forged check case, for example, the fingerprint of a suspect on a check would be considered very damaging evidence that cannot be easily explained away.

Determination of plausible or legal access to a document is not within the expertise of a document examiner.

A survey has shown that most large police departments in North America and Western Europe process bogus checks for fingerprints. The philosophy is that a modern police department must collect all available evidence to a crime – particularly evidence such as fingerprints, which is readily accepted in courts of law. Although handwriting evidence in a check case can be sufficient to convict a suspect, it is generally felt that additional fingerprint evidence can only assist the prosecution.

Sometimes fingerprints on paper are quite visible to the naked eye, either with or without special types of lighting. If such is the case, those prints should be photographed. Today there are also numerous scientific methods to develop prints on documents. Some of the more popular methods are described below.

BIBLIOGRAPHY – GENERAL

Conway, James V.P. (1965), "Fingerprints and Documents," Paper presented at the annual meeting of the American Society of Questioned Document Examiners, Ottawa, Ontario.

UK Home Office Police Scientific Development Branch (1998), *Manual of Fingerprint Development Techniques: Guide to the Selection and Use of Processes for the Development of Latent Fingerprints*, 2nd edn, Sandridge, UK.

ORDINARY FLUORESCENCE EXAMINATION

Some of the materials in fingerprints as well as environmental contaminants can fluoresce; however this is almost always better after treatment. Viewing fluorescence before scientific treatment should be considered as preliminary (unless, of course, the desired fingerprint is visible). Note that a proper fluorescence search can be quite time consuming.

When photographing fluorescence with an argon laser, it is best to use 488 nm or 514.5 nm. When using ninhydrin the following wavelengths are also recommended: 457.9 nm, 476.5 nm. Gentian violet requires 528.7 nm.

DFO (1,8-DIAZAFLUOREN-9-ONE)

DFO is the single most effective reagent to develop fingerprints on paper and porous surfaces. Resultant fingerprints fluoresce, and they are not generally seen with visible light. For this reason many laboratories use ninhydrin. For best results a high intensity light source should be used.

If both DFO and ninhydrin are used, DFO should be tried first. Ninhydrin has the potential of developing additional prints after DFO is used. DFO should be used *after* handwriting and indented writing (ESDA) examinations. Proper procedure is to use DFO when wearing protective gear in a properly ventilated environment.

NINHYDRIN ($C_9H_6O_4$)

The use of ninhydrin for fingerprint development began in the 1950s and has been since the 1960s the most popular method used to develop latent fingerprints on paper. Its advantages are low cost and simplicity of use. These factors outweigh the use of DFO, even though the latter is more effective in recovering latent prints on paper.

A ninhydrin spray can either be prepared (acetic acid, ethanol, freon, and ninhydrin) or purchased in ready-made spray cans. In-house preparation of a ninhydrin bath is usually done by high-volume users who are looking to cut operating costs.

It is best to examine handwriting using plastic covering, then process with ninhydrin. Any ESDA examination should also be done before ninhydrin is used. Documents should be photographed before processing with ninhydrin, and fingerprints retrieved should also be photographed because of possible fading. Zinc toning solution is sometimes used to provide a contrasting color or to enhance results, especially when dealing with blood.

Processing with ninhydrin does not preclude usual handwriting or other technical examinations, although it *does* leave purple stains (Ruhemann's Purple) on the document, which some examiners view as a hindrance. In the early period of ninhydrin use for fingerprints there often was significant "bleeding" of ink. Current formulations of ninhydrin keep this phenomenon to a minimum but it is still to be found.

It has been shown that ninhydrin has been used successfully to develop fingerprints left on paper not just months but years previously. Humidification enhances results and speeds development of prints. Ninhydrin should be used only with proper ventilation.

Although most fingerprints develop with ninhydrin almost immediately, a small number of prints can develop over a period of up to more than one week.

BIBLIOGRAPHY – NINHYDRIN

Crown, David A. (1963), "Non-Polar Solutions of Ninhydrin for Developing Latent Fingerprints," Paper presented at the annual meeting of the American Society of Questioned Document Examiners, Washington, DC.

Kobus, H.J. *et al.* (1983), "A Simple Luminescent Post-Ninhydrin Treatment for the Improved Visualisation of Fingerprints on Documents in Cases Where Ninhydrin Alone Gives Poor Results," *Forensic Science International*, 22(2–3): 161–170.

POWDERS

Powders can be used to develop fingerprints on paper, but they tend to be insensitive to older prints. There are several different types of powders which can be applied to develop fingerprints:

- aluminum
- conventional
- magnetic (generally less sensitive except on glossy paper)
- fluorescent

When using powders, a brush is required. The recommended model is glass fiber with carbon fiber following, though more ordinary brushes are generally satisfactory with fluorescent powders.

CYANOACRYLATE VAPOR

One of the most effective and easy-to-use methods to develop fingerprints on paper and other surfaces is ethyl cyanoacrylate vapor (also known under the commercial name, Superglue®) used in conjunction with a fluorescent dye. The document on which fingerprints are sought is exposed in a proper chamber (air-tight, internal air system to provide even air flow, ventilation in the general area). Maximum results are obtained at room temperature with a humidity of

80% and cyanoacrylate heated to 120°C. Cyanoacrylate should be used after ink, paper and ESDA® examinations. Cyanoacrylite can be used by trained technicians.

PHYSICAL DEVELOPER (PD)

Physical developer (silver-based aqueous reagent) can be used to develop fingerprints on paper after ninhydrin and FDO have been used. PD should be used after ink, paper and ESDA® examinations. It can be used on dry paper; however best results are from wet paper.

NOTE ON OTHER METHODS

There are several other methods which are theoretically possible to use but for various reasons they are not commonly tried:

- ESDA – although fingerprints can be developed by this method, ESDA is much less sensitive than more standard fingerprint procedures.
- Radioactive sulfur dioxide or radioactive thiourea/sodium hydroxide solution – not generally available and to be used only in working environments specially approved for the purpose.

IN CONCLUSION

Even if all known fingerprint development methods are used and a particular print is not found, inference *absolutely* cannot be made that said person did not touch the document in question at some point in time. If fingerprints *are* found, it cannot be determined when that person touched the document.

Historically, some laboratories searched for fingerprints before handwriting was examined. Today, this is no longer recommended, since certain latent fingerprint methods preclude technical examinations such as ESDA (see above).

Q. Did Mr X touch the document in question?
A. His fingerprints were not found on the document.

Q. Can we infer from this that he never handled the document?
A. No, that cannot be inferred. To be exact, his fingerprints were not found on the document. Or, in other words, I have found no evidence that he touched the document.

Q. Could he have touched the document?
A. The fact that fingerprints are not found on a document does not preclude the possibility that someone touched the document.

Q. Let us rephrase so there is no misunderstanding. Is it possible that Mr X handled the document in question even though you did not find his fingerprints?
A. Yes, the fact that I did not find his fingerprints does not prove that he did not handle the document.

CHAPTER 15

EXAMINATION EQUIPMENT

LIGHT SOURCES

UV

Many documents have a specific look when viewed under ultra-violet light. Many security papers, for example, show a special design or tint. Security inks can show a special color under ultra-violet.

To make a complete examination, both long (366.3 m) and short wave (253.7 m) UV should be used.

A difference under UV in two inks, papers, etc. is sufficient to say that they are different. (Since ink can react with paper, either unused ink or samples on the same paper should be used where possible.) To record UV findings on film, Wratten filter 18A is recommended for reflected UV photography; No. 2A is recommended for fluorescent photography.

A word of caution: it can be harmful to the eye to look directly into a UV light source. One should look only at reflected light unless protective glasses are worn.

IR

IR can be used to differentiate between colors of ink. In simple terms, this means that: (a) text written in two different inks can be separated, (b) alterations can be identified, and (c) in some cases erased text can be restored.

An important feature of any apparatus is an IR light source from below the document. This is important to check such matters as the text under correction fluids such as "Typex[1]" and the presence of writing such as "Photo of Bearer" under passport pictures. In certain cases it can also be used to read letters in sealed envelopes.

A number of different wratten filters can be used with IR films, however for document examination No. 87 has been found most effective for documents work (with IR film); No. 25 is recommended as a good general IR film. When using Wratten No. 87 it should be remembered that double the exposure time is needed as for No. 25.

[1] Correction materials have varied historically. One of the early modern correction methods was an over-write tape inserted between a typewriter ribbon and the paper/platen (separate tape for carbon copy correction). This was then modified by the IBM Selectric II with the tape controlled by the typewriter. Fluids are both the type requiring a thinner and those which do not need such. Layover tapes and layover levels have also been used. In virtually all of these cases the original text can be deciphered using IR light from below. This method is not effective with very thick papers such as cardboard.

Figure 15.1 (a and b)

One signature is written over another. Using IR the original signature is readable. (Courtesy of Yaacov Yaniv, Jerusalem, Israel)

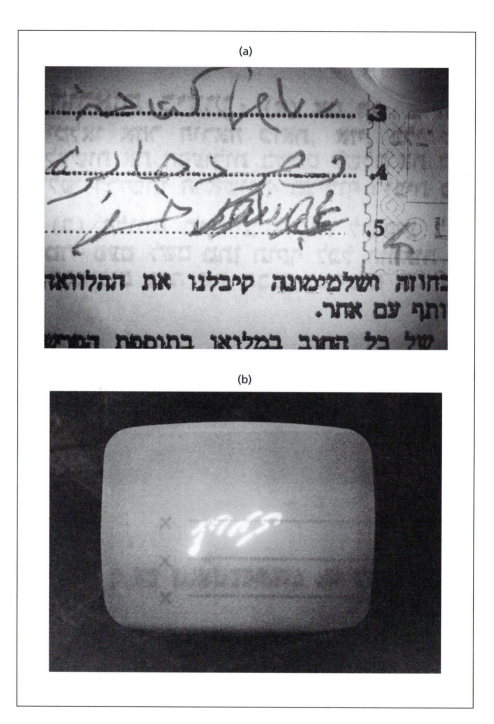

IRL

IRL was introduced into the examination of Questioned Documents by Linton Godown in the late 1950s. This luminescence is a fluorescence emitted in the near infra-red range (700 nm to 2000 nm) by a light source of lower wavelength than 700 nm.

The basic use of IRL is for the differentiation of inks and for restoration. Godown's method was to illuminate a document with an incandescent light source covered by a filter of 5 to 10% solution copper sulfate ($CuSO_2$) housed in a 1 cm thick chamber. This chamber is then covered with a filter (e.g. Wratten 2A, 4, 22 or 29). Filters (e.g. Wratten 87, 87C, 88A or 89B) are then placed over the lens of the camera which is loaded with IR film. This procedure is long and complicated. Today the VSC (manufactured by Foster and Freeman Ltd) has an IRL capability virtually at the flip of a switch.

A case has also been made for viewing IR and IRL results on a CCTV (closed circuit television) system. This has shown positive results on specialized examinations. As of this writing, however, use of CCTV is not to be found in very many laboratories.

BIBLIOGRAPHY

Ellen, David M. and Creer, Ken E. (1970), "Infrared Luminescence in the Examination of Documents," *Journal of the Forensic Science Society*, 10(3) (July): 159–164.

Hoover, Herbert L. and MacDonell, Herbert L. (1964), "Infrared Luminescence Using Glass Filters," *American Journal of Forensic Sciences*, 9(1): 89–98.

Kayser, J. Ferdinand (1966), "Some Fallacies about the Photography of Luminescence," *Medicine, Science and the Law*, 9(1): 45–46.

ESDA®[2]

The purpose of this type of machine, such as the model developed by Foster and Morantz in work carried out at the London College of Printing and introduced in 1979, is to develop indented writing on a document. Previously the most commonly accepted methods of detecting such writing included the use of side lighting, fluorescent powder, Ronchi plate, sulfur dioxide, benzene evaporation, radiology, and iodine fuming. In most cases ESDA (Electro Static Detection Apparatus) provided a much more effective tool that is simpler and quicker to use. This, however, is not always the case, and there is ample reason to try alternative methods when ESDA does not yield the desired results.

A by-product of ESDA is that it can detect indentations not necessarily caused

2 *ESDA® is a commercial product sold by Foster and Freeman (UK). The term is used to cover all machines of this type. The Hungarian Police, for example, developed a homemade "ESDA" machine that showed impressive results. Lightning Powder Company (USA) also markets a similar instrument under the name "VacuBox."*

by the direct writing process (such as by secret writing, erasure and alteration).

The basic principle of the machine is that when a document is held against a polymer sheet (e.g. Milar®) on one side and a bronze plate on the other, a capacitor is formed with the document serving as the dielectric. (A pump is included in the ESDA to assure strong adherence of the polymer to the document.) When a corona with a positive electrical field is moved over the document, electrons are drawn off the surface of the document in proportion to the document thickness. Thus, where there is an indentation, more charge will be stored. If negative toner is applied (ESDA has two alternative methods: cascade developer and powder cloud), there is a stronger attraction of the toner to those indented areas.

Indented handwriting developed by an ESDA machine can be examined to determine the identity of the writer; however, results are limited by the quality of the text recovered. One limiting factor always present is the lack of ink (hence pen striations reflected in the ink).

Humidity enhances the possibilities of an ESDA image, hence a humidity chamber is part of the apparatus. At least one test has shown that an ESDA machine kept in a humid working environment has also shown better results. On the other hand, excessive humidity has shown poorer results.

ESDA has been shown to be effective in developing writing indentation on historical documents more than fifty years old. This is, of course, very much dependent on the manner in which documents were handled and stored.

Certain chemicals applied to the page to be examined preclude ESDA images. These chemicals include methanol, acetone, flurisol and petroleum ether. This should be remembered when using one of these chemicals for latent fingerprint development.

Often the image restored by ESDA is partial or has traces of writing which are not readily deciphered. To deal with these problems there have been attempts to use computer software for image enhancement. Computer imaging and photographic systems have been used to separate different layers of writing (e.g. the impressions left from writing three documents on the same pad); here care should be taken that the examiner does not select writing without true justification.

In cases where ESDA does not restore indented writing, there has been success using photography with argon ion and other lasers together with the use of filters.

BIBLIOGRAPHY

Baier, Peter E. and Teder, Wolfgang (1988), "ESDA – Improvements by Computer Assistance," Paper presented at the annual meeting of the American Society of Questioned Document Examiners, Denver, Colorado.

Ellen, David M., Foster, D.J. and Morantz, D.J. (1980), "The Use of Electrostatic Imaging in the Detection of Indented Impressions," *Forensic Science International*, 15: 53–60.

Foster, D.J. and Morantz, D.J. (1979), "An Electrostatic Imaging Technique for the Detection of Indented Impressions in Documents," *Forensic Science International*, 13: 51–54.

Lewis, George W. (1981), "Examining Indented Writings using the Electrostatic Detection Apparatus (ESDA)," Paper presented at the annual meeting of the American Society of Questioned Document Examiners, Houston, Texas.

BIBLIOGRAPHY – ALTERNATIVES TO ESDA FOR INDENTATIONS

Brown, Jerry L. (1998), "Survey of Techniques used to Visualize Indented Markings," *Journal of the American Society of Questioned Document Examiners*, 1(2): 107–112.

MAGNIFIERS

For reasons of convenience many document examiners have a series of magnification glasses in addition to a standard magnifier which, if raised and lowered to change magnification, can distort the image being viewed. (Typical distortion is "bellowing" around the edges, lack of clarity, disproportion, and false colors.)

MICROSCOPES

Standard laboratory microscopes are of the light microscope variety, based on the invention of Anton van Leeuwenhoek in the seventeenth century. In this type of microscope the initial source is light, rather than an electron source. Laboratory microscopes are usually compound; these come in both monocular and binocular versions, where the former has one eye piece and the latter has eye pieces for both eyes (though not stereo vision). Although the same images can be seen with either system, the binocular version is much easier to use.

The general distortions found in microscopes are spherical and chromatic, resulting in hazy images and a reduction in contrast, or problems with seeing certain colors.

A microscope is a key instrument in document examination, since it allows an examiner to view detail not seen with a hand magnifier. This is particularly important in certain examinations to determine method of printing or even authorship of handwriting. It is absolutely appropriate for a lawyer to verify in court that an examiner had a microscope at his disposal during an examination. (Note that virtually all government laboratories are equipped with appropriate microscopes. Equipment problems, in general, are more often found among private examiners.)

Although an electron microscope has strong resolution, its strength of magnification is usually beyond the needs of a document examiner unless there is an unusual examination (e.g. paper fibers). Then the resolution can be helpful to identify small particles, which can be isolated. (In a SEM [scanning electron microscope] this is done in conjunction with a computer program.)

A special attachment to a microscope is needed for photography. An alternative to photographing through the lens of a microscope is to use a camera that has a long bellows, an appropriate short focus lens, and a large enough sheet of film. Enlargements of up to 20 or 25 times can be made using this procedure.

BIBLIOGRAPHY

Black, David A. (1952), "The Microscope in Document Examination," *Journal of Criminology and Police Science*, 42: 310–320.

PROJECTINA®

The classic Projectina apparatus allowed the enlargement, side-by-side comparison, and super-imposition of two still images. (Superimposition is achieved by alternating flickering images at the rate of 0 to 8 per second.) More modern versions of the Projectina also include accessories for UV and IR, and for 35 mm photography.

The method certainly has its advantages; however, particularly in older models blowing of vented air sometimes caused slight "dancing" of images and the resolution is far from that of photographic images. It can be said that although the Projectina may be convenient to use for comparison (instead of photographing and comparing the prints or overlaying negatives), it is far from being irreplaceable. A documents laboratory without a Projectina can still be called well equipped.

In recent years Projectina has marketed several light sources and the FRS II Film Ribbon Scanner. The purpose of the latter is to feed the ribbon being examined through a holder and focus the image upon a video screen. Although this method is certainly comfortable, it is no more effective than slowly feeding the ribbon over a light table. Promised software for automatic interpretation has yet to be introduced to the market.

LASER

Although the argon laser has been best known since 1976 for its application to fingerprints, attempts have been made to apply it to document examination. The most productive lines for document work have been found to be 514.5 nm and 488 nm with Wratten filters 15 and 22.

Basic uses of the argon laser are to read erased entries and to differentiate between inks. The laser has also been used to find fingerprints on paper without destroying the document. Advocates of laser technology claim that results with the laser are superior to regular sources of luminescence.

BIBLIOGRAPHY

Creer, Ken (1981), "Use of an Argon Ion Laser in the Examination of Questioned Documents," Paper presented at International Association of Forensic Sciences.

CHAPTER 16

EXAMPLES OF MATERIALS
TO BE EXAMINED

INTRODUCTION

There is no limit to the materials that a document examiner can receive for examination. This chapter, however, gives illustrations of some of the most commonly encountered items and the problems inherent therein.

PASSPORTS

Since the First World War passports as we know them today (small bound booklets with personalia, issuance, and travel pages) have been the common and accepted means of personal identification for international travel. The United States first required passports of foreign travelers in 1918. There are numerous basic types of passports in current international use today:

- Passports for citizens: *tourist* (issued to citizens for their personal travel; a special document is issued by Israel to new citizens), *service* or *official* (issued to government employees on official travel), and *diplomatic* (issued to Ministry of Foreign Affairs personnel with diplomatic status).
- Travel documents for permanent residents and other non-citizens: *laissez-passer* (a document identifying an individual for travel purposes), and *Passport for Palestinians* (issued by certain Arab countries to identify Palestinians for purposes of travel).

A valid passport is not necessarily sufficient documentation for international travel. Certain countries require that nationals of other specified countries obtain a visa prior to entry. Once again, there are several different types of visas (tourist, student, business, clergy, immigrant, etc.).

In many countries passports are stamped with cachets upon border entry and border exit. In some countries special cachets are used to denote that the person presented himself at border control, but entry into the country was denied. (In Israel a common question in the police caseload has been intentional destruction or mutilation of a passport when a denial cachet is present. The guiding rule is that it is not an offense to be denied entry to a foreign country, but it is an offense in Israel to intentionally damage an Israeli passport. If a passport is mutilated by laundry, the document examiner can guess regarding intention, but he cannot prove his position. There is a better chance to prove intentional mutilation by page removal or excess inking; however, even here much of the evidence can be only circumstantial.)

SECURITY FEATURES

The modern passports of most countries are sophisticated documents which have a number of features designed to thwart attempts of fraud.

- *Cover.* This is usually of a material with a specific grain or pattern unavailable on the commercial market and onto which is impressed both text and a design (usually a country seal).
- *Binding.* A specific number and pattern of stitches, usually with a specific thread, can be effective in preventing disassembly of the passport, page substitution, and resewing.
- *Paper.* Today virtually all passports are printed on paper containing some type of watermark which is not available on the commercial market. Sometimes security threads or fibers are included in the paper.
- *Printing.* A well-designed passport will be printed with a background tint of delicate design appearing in a color difficult to photograph with fine detail for offset printing. Guilloches and latent images are also common. Special inks with ultraviolet or infrared quality are also often used to enhance security, prevent duplication, and show attempts at alteration.
- *Photograph.* Numerous methods have been used to fasten the photograph to the page, thus making photo substitution more difficult. These methods vary from plastic overlays (sometimes with a retro-reflective design) or imprinting text ("tying" the photo to the page), to the use of special grommets. When a plastic mold cachet is impressed it should be remembered that the height of the photograph off the page can cause distortion in the impression. Likewise, due to the influence of chemicals in the photograph paper, a "difference" of ink color can sometimes be perceived.

These are only some of the security devices available. There are numerous others, including special marks, coded numbers, etc.

TYPES OF FORGERY

There are numerous different types of passports in circulation today. Most of these documents are of the tourist passport type.

- *Altered genuine documents.* This usually entails photograph substitution to enable use of the document by other than the legal bearer; it can also include page substitution. (The most frequent substitutions are either to change the personalia pages or to add a page with a genuine visa, which originally had been entered in another passport. An alternative method is to use a genuine visa page, usually from another passport of the same series, and prepare it as a personalia page; in this case the page should be examined for erased or hidden original text as well as printing/fill-in irregularities of personalia details.)

   Other examples of passport alterations are "extending" the validity of the document by changing the date of expiration and removing or rendering illegible any visa refusal, entrance denial, or expulsion notations.

- *Total forgery.* "Issuance" to an individual of a totally forged passport (usually for the purpose of illegal immigration or terrorism, but these forgeries have also been seen in connection with usually low level drug trade).
- *Stolen blank.* These are genuinely printed documents which are stolen from official offices, while still blank, then "issued" to illegal travelers.
- *Notional.* Several international organizations have sold "passports" expounding upon the right of every person to freedom of travel. There are also some notional versions of national passports (with no relation to the original authentic document).
- *Illegal supporting papers.* It is estimated that in the United States the most common type of illegally held passport is a genuine document officially issued, but on the basis of fraudulent supporting papers (voting permit, birth certificate[1], etc.). (In this case the document examiner might be called upon to examine the supporting papers, but not the resultant and quite genuine passport.)

[1] *See section later in this chapter on birth certificates.*

CASE LOAD

The average document examiner, particularly in the private sector, has a major problem examining passports because of the lack of adequate comparative materials. There are hundreds of passport versions in circulation today, and acquiring the proper specimen for comparative examination can be more than a simple chore. This problem is only compounded when talking about examination of visas and border cachets.

BIBLIOGRAPHY – EXAMINATION

Al-Jabour, Mohammad Odeh (1988), *The Fight against Passport and Travel Documentation Forgery* (in Arabic), Arab Center for Security Studies and Training, Riyadh, Saudi Arabia.

Levinson, Jay (1984), "Passport Examination," *Journal of Forensic Sciences*, 29(2): 628–632.

McCarthy, William, Jr and Larner, James F. (1987), "Forensic Examination of a Passport," Paper presented at the International Association of Forensic Sciences, Vancouver, British Columbia.

BIBLIOGRAPHY – PASSPORT GUIDES

Henny, David (1989 and updates), *Passport Handbook to Check the Authenticity of Passports*, Kluwerpers, Utrecht, Netherlands.

Interpol, *Annual Passport Guide: Passports and ID-Cards of Europe and a Selection of Other Countries*, Keesing Security Documents Publishing BV, Amsterdam, Netherlands. (Relatively few identity cards are included, and country coverage outside Europe is erratic. Although the volume begins with an introduction to security features, the country sections are without reference to these security features. Good as a general identification tool, but (as stated in the volume) not necessarily covering all passports in current use.)

IDENTITY CARDS

When an Israeli identification card (Hebrew *te'udat zehut*, Arabic *hawiyya*) is submitted for examination, the question is usually whether there has been photo substitution, although there have been some forged printings of the document. The method to determine photo substitution is to examine the plastic cover over the photograph to see whether it has been removed. If the answer is positive, proof of illegal intent must be brought by showing either fibers from a previous photograph or tears in the identity card which could not have been made by either the plastic covering sheet or the existing photograph and its glue.

For the record it should be noted that particularly in the booklet style identity cards the plastic sheet over the picture was known to come loose after extensive humidity, use, bending, etc. That version has now been replaced by a laminated card and a page of changing family details (children under 18) printed on security paper.

SIGNATURES ON ART

Every painter has his own style of signature. By this it is meant not only style in the graphic sense, but also placement and materials. Although the medium is quite different from the usual document, many of the standard principles of signature examination still apply. In cases of forgery the examiner should be alert to the possibility that the original signature was scraped from the canvas or covered and repainted.

This is a very specialized area of document examination, and one in which not many examiners have any experience. In no way should the examiner's role be confused with that of the art expert. It is not the function of the document examiner to decide questions of painting style.

BIBLIOGRAPHY

Goetschel, Corinne (1988), "Problem of Identifying Disputed Signatures on Works of Art," Paper presented at the annual meeting of the American Society of Questioned Document Examiners, Denver, Colorado.

Widla, Tadeusz (1985), "Forgery of Artists' Signatures," Paper presented at *Experiencing Graphology '85*, Jerusalem, Israel.

CURRENCY

Forgery of currency is by no means a new phenomenon. One might say rather facetiously that it is a compliment to monetary stability when currency is forged. When a country experiences rampant inflation, it is rare that its currency is printed in counterfeit.

Today the counterfeit bank note most commonly encountered in European countries in more sophisticated forgeries is United States currency. Unlike generally circulated statistics according to which $10 and $20 notes account for 71% of all US currency forgeries, abroad it is the $100 note that is most commonly encountered as a forgery. In many countries counterfeit US dollars are more commonly encountered than bogus local currency because of relatively less familiarity with the security features of the currency.

Most counterfeit notes passed in smaller countries are printed abroad and brought in either by unwitting tourists (usually unfamiliar with dollar notes and receiving them in "unofficial" currency transactions prior to a voyage), or by persons having criminal intent. Although most forgeries tend to be notes printed relatively recently, a marked percentage of the counterfeit notes detected are older notes which show signs of having been in circulation. There also have been cases of US counterfeit currency forgeries produced in a long list of foreign countries.

International experience has shown that very few counterfeiters work alone. The most common method of counterfeit money production is for several people to "commission" a printing as an investment. Then, technicians are hired, each to perform a different part of the work. From the criminal's point of view this compartmentation further limits vulnerability of the operation to police penetration, since the most visible parts are unaware of who is really behind the forgery.

The United States dollar is not the only counterfeit note circulation. There have been forgeries of the Jordanian dinar, English pound sterling, French franc, German Mark, and others that have been detected.

Currency forgeries are usually photo offset printings or color photocopies[2], sometimes with the added enhancement that the serial number is printed by

[2] *Drawn forgeries have been produced, but they are extremely rare and generally of poor quality. For an example, see C.T. Symons, "Ultra-Violet Light in Criminal Investigation," Police Journal, 3(2) (April 1930): 238.*

letterpress or typography. The basic reason is the ready availability of offset equipment and the fact that virtually all modern printers have been trained in offset.

Monochrome photocopied notes with color added by pencil, color photocopies, and totally hand-drawn forgeries have also been detected. As could be expected, there is a wide variation in the "quality" of the forgeries. In recent years there has been a sharp increase in the number of forgeries produced by color photocopies, since these machines are relatively less expensive and more readily available than in the past.

Figure 16.1

Photocopied forgery of Jordanian 10 Dinar note. The forgery lacks detail and appropriate color. The watermark was printed.

In many foreign countries special currency units rather than the questioned documents laboratory handle cases. In other countries, however, this is considered a documents laboratory function.

A typical question asked of expert witnesses in court is designed to gage the sophistication of the forgery. The proper answer to be given is that it is not the role of a document examiner to estimate a layman's technical familiarity with currency notes and his ability to draw professional conclusions.

Q.   Would you say that this is a particularly sophisticated forgery?

A.   It is not within the realm of my expertise to rate sophistication. As I said, this is a forgery.

Q.   Could the average person determine that this is a forgery?

A.   I am a trained document examiner, and I determined it is a forgery. I really cannot speak for anyone other than myself.

Q.   My client has been charged with passing counterfeit currency. Isn't it possible that he did not realize that these notes were counterfeit?

A.   It is not within the realm of my expertise to determine what your client did or did not know. I can only repeat my testimony that the currency in question is counterfeit.

In one case involving misrepresentation, not forgery, authentic but demonetized Cambodian bank notes of a government formerly in power were passed as West German marks.

The primary international system to classify forgeries is that of Interpol. The forged notes of each country are classified and pictured, highlighting mistakes and defects in the printing. It should be noted that the Interpol system, particularly in the case of US currency, shows printing plate numbers and not serial numbers, since most forgers are well aware of the need to vary serial numbers.

Interpol counterfeit currency notices are printed and circulated periodically to subscribing police organizations. It is standard police practice in many countries to record the Interpol number (if existing) of counterfeit currency found in document examination cases.

UNITED STATES GENUINE CURRENCY

Although United States currency notes are all printed in variations of a basic green, there are numerous features which make the notes extremely difficult to forge, particularly in its new format.

A basic principle in the examination of United States currency (and many other major currencies) is that printing and production quality control is so strict that sub-standard notes and printing errors are always caught during the various stages of production; these notes are never released to the public. Printing is also done from steel plates allowing a much greater amount of fine detail than can be reproduced photographically or imitated using less technical methods.

Many countries with sub-standard local printing facilities contract out currency printing to foreign companies, thus better insuring a quality product.

The paper in United States currency is pure white with small and colored silk fibers added to the pulp during the manufacturing process. These fibers are part of the paper; in forgeries they are often color-penciled in or printed on the note.

On 10 July 1929 the "new series" smaller sized currency was first introduced, and today it is becoming extremely rare to find any of the 1928 printed notes in circulation. (Old series notes no longer circulate. They retain their legal value but the value to a collector is much greater than in the bank.) The basic "new series" notes have remained quite standard; however, there have been certain changes over the years (Table 16.1).

Table 16.1

Changes to "new series" bank notes

Year	Change
1950	Black Federal Reserve regional seals made smaller and surrounded by sharp points
1954	Addition of "In God We Trust"
Early 1950s	Introduction of magnetic ink
1971	Only Federal Reserve Notes are issued

Many banks have purchased machines to "detect" counterfeit United States currency. The working principle of one type of these machines is to sound a pulse when magnetic ink (containing iron oxide) is found. Thus, since such ink was first introduced in the early 1950s, a false indication of forgery is often encountered for older notes.

Another false indication with forgeries is the condition of the note. Quite often a note will show the signs of use ("slickness," dirt hiding security fibers, appearance of "washed" colors). It should be remembered that use, alone, is no indication of authenticity, since there have been cases of counterfeit notes circulating extensively before being caught. One technique used by some forgers is to artificially age notes to give the appearance of use. Typical methods would be to fold or crease, or to pass from hand to hand.

In addition to totally counterfeit notes there have been instances when genuine notes were "raised." For example, $1 notes have been washed or pasted to raise the value to higher sums. A basic method of detection is to ascertain that the proper portrait appears on the note.

Table 16.2

Commonly encountered notes

Denomination ($)	Portrait	Reverse
1	Washington	Great Seal of the US
2	Jefferson	Monticello (until 1966) Declaration of Independence (from April 1976)
5	Lincoln	Memorial
10	Hamilton	US Treasury Building
20	Jackson	White House
50	Grant	US Capitol
100	Franklin	Independence Hall

Notes of larger denominations were printed prior to 1945, however they are no longer in general circulation. Some very large notes were printed in such limited quantities that they are only a technical footnote to valid currency lists.

Each note has a serial number consisting of a letter prefix, eight digits, and a letter suffix. Since 1928 all notes except National Bank Notes contain a black check letter selected from "A" to "R". Since 1963 when printing in sheets of 32 was introduced, all notes contain a "quadrant number," from A to H and from 1 to 4; thus, G3 locates the specific printing quadrant. On the front and verso of the note there are also plate numbers. Since 26 April 1991 the Western Currency Facility has been operating in Fort Worth, Texas. Notes printed at this facility have the letters FW preceding the quadrant number, such as FWA1.

A common question asked about currency notes is the meaning of the color on the face of the note in the seal and serial number. This color relates to the technical backing of the note (Table 16.3).

Treasury Seal & Serial number	Type	Denomination ($)
Green	Federal Reserve	1, 2, 5, 10, 20, 50, 100
Red	US Notes	2, 5, 100
Blue	Silver Certificates	1, 5, 10

Table 16.3
Color of seal and serial number, and its meaning

Special currency was issued for emergency use during the Second World War. This includes several varieties of notes (silver certificates with gold seal, national currency with brown seals, Hawaii overprints); today, however, they are all collectors' pieces.

Silver certificates and United States Notes in $2 and $5 denominations are no longer being printed.

Federal Reserve Notes are issued by one of twelve banks in the United States. Each currency note shows both the bank name and its numeric and alphabetic codes (Table 16.4). Any deviation from standard codes is proof of forgery.

Code	Bank	Code	Bank
1-A	Boston	7-G	Chicago
2-B	New York	8-H	St. Louis
3-C	Philadelphia	9-I	Minneapolis
4-D	Cleveland	10-J	Kansas City
5-E	Richmond	11-K	Dallas
6-F	Atlanta	12-L	San Francisco

Table 16.4
Federal Reserve Banks and Codes

The United States Department of Treasury announced plans to introduce new security features into its currency beginning in the early 1990s. The $100 bill was presented in August 1991, $50 in March 1992, $20 in October 1992, and $10 the following month.

A program was then developed to introduce these newly designed notes with increased security guards. These features include microprinting of text as part of the picture and a watermark picturing the person in the portrait on the note. The new $100 note was released in 1996; the $50 note was released in 1997; the $20 note was released in 1998. Release of $10 and $5 notes is projected for the summer of 2000. Color-shifting ink (patented by Optical Coating Laboratory/Flex Products of California) is used on these notes. Certain colors shift from green to black according to the angle of view.

BIBLIOGRAPHY

Nepote, Jean (1980), "Currency Counterfeiting," *International Criminal Police Review*, no. 341: 210–217.

United States Secret Service, *Know Your Money*, United States Government Printing Office, Washington, DC (numerous printings)[3].

[3] *Initial American (and British) policy was to ignore counterfeit currency in public, thinking that mention of the subject would be detrimental, either causing lack of confidence in currency or teaching forgers to correct their mistakes. The "Know Your Money" concept was started by the Secret Service under the direction of Frank J. Wilson in 1937, and a booklet describing currency security features was published.*

OTHER CURRENCY

Many countries use security threads in their currency. These polyester threads, usually 0.5 mm wide, are incorporated into the paper during manufacture. There are very few papermills which have the appropriate technology, and reproducing these threads is well beyond the capability of the usual counterfeiter. The threads can be classified into groups: visual characteristics (color, printed text [under magnification]), and machine readable qualities (metallic features, fluorescent threads).

There have also been instances in which coins and tokens have been counterfeited. Bogus coins were known even in ancient times. Although forgery is most common with coins of great value, such as gold pieces or rare coins, this has extended even to ordinary coinage (higher value coins).

In recent years there has been a decline in the use of bogus tokens given the prevalence of other methods of payment (such as telephone cards which have eliminated the use of telephone tokens in many countries).

Ninhydrin followed by physical developer can develop fingerprints on relatively new currency notes. There is generally no point in trying to develop fingerprints on currency that has seen extensive circulation.

CREDIT CARDS

Credit cards have been in popular circulation since the early post-Second World War period. Originally they were metal, but since the 1960s a plastic version has been the standard. In many developing countries, however, domestically issued credit cards first started in the mid-1970s. There are still many countries which even at the end of the twentieth century do not use credit cards very extensively.

In many countries the cards loosely called "credit cards" are, in fact, debit cards. A credit card allows the bearer to use his credit and schedule his payments. With debit cards the outstanding balance is deducted or debited from the bearer's bank account at fixed intervals. Only recently have debit cards become popular in North America.

By looking at a card it is impossible to know if it is a credit card or a debit card. The nature of the card is governed by the agreement between bearer and bank.

Most credit cards also double as machine teller (ATM-type) instruments. The card is placed into a slot at an automatic teller, and the bearer is requested to enter his code number (in fact a number related by a pre-set formula to the number stored in the metallic strip on the reverse of the card). There are banks which issue cards valid only in ATM machines for controlled transactions and not for market purchases.

In some countries it was common practice for certain companies to issue their own cards, thus having better control over usage and over stolen/lost reports. This practice has most often been replaced by the multi-purpose card issued by a central bank/credit company, which has been more cost-effective despite a certain amount of financial loss.

CARD PRODUCTION

Although card production is not an overly technical procedure, aspects of market competition have caused a situation where card manufacturers sell blanks to card issuance companies. Fill-in of specific cards is then accomplished by the direct issuance company.

The cards have a core of polyvinyl chloride which is sandwiched between clear sheets under heavy pressure.

The impressed letters on the cards are entered by a machine operating on the principle of pressure. Heat would cause the card to buckle; it would also disturb the background design. In some forgeries the genuine card *is* heated to "erase" the numbers/name and replace them with other information. The alterations can usually be detected based upon this buckling or disturbed background or the presence of small metal deposits left as part of the heating process.

The approved typestyle for the encoded line with account number is

Farrington 7B, an OCR (optical character recognition) font. The cards are usually 0.030″ thick. Standard sizes are CR50 (3.50″ × 1.725″) and CR80 (3.75″ × 2.125″).

The bearer is supposed to sign the card upon receipt so that his signature can be compared at the time of transaction. Store clerks, however, are certainly not document examiners, and in reality they are in no position to undertake signature comparisons. (It should also be observed that because the signature strip is relatively small, the writing of certain people is necessarily distorted.) This stage is also often overlooked as store clerks pass the card through a reader, relying on "the system" to catch bad cards, rather than signature verification.

Even document examiners can have a difficult time verifying the signatures on credit card receipts, due to the limited space for writing and often awkward writing positions (e.g. standing with packages, sitting in a cramped position behind a car steering wheel). Commercial vendors are also in a poor position to do any but the most elementary comparison of picture on the credit card to the bearer. This is due to factors such a clothing, age of photograph, cash register pressure, and the basic reality that most credit card companies guarantee payment unless the card number is on a black list (nowadays most often computer-searched).

For certain transactions a coded number (PIN – personal identification number) is entered into a machine. This number is then compared by mathematical formula to a number in a metallic strip on the verso of the card. Mathematical "matches" validate the transaction.

To increase security a hologram (three-dimensional) image has been added to most major cards. In many instances there is often a special character (usually a company symbol) as part of the raised lettering of the card.

TYPES OF FRAUD

There are numerous types of credit card fraud which have been committed:

- *Total forgery.* This type of forgery has been relatively rare in recent years despite the abundance of credit cards to be found that do not have the security devices of multi-purpose cards. The basic problems in producing total forgeries are the costs involved and on-line checking of cards at the point of purchase. Even when checking is against a black-list rather than verification, the procedure limits the amount of time a card can be used safely by the forger.
- *Stolen/lost.* This is the most common credit card fraud, since no costs are involved (unless details on the card are changed [usually by a thermal process]). Most users of stolen cards are aware that lost/stolen black-lists are regional, hence using the card far from the point of issue or from the owner's residence decreases the possibility of discovery.

- *Genuine card based on illegal client identification.* This type of fraud allows the card owner to obtain a card by giving false information, then using it with no fear of want lists. The card becomes too "hot" only after payment to the company becomes delinquent. The problems involved here are similar to those involved in obtaining a passport based upon spurious supporting documentation.

- *Altered.* In this case a genuine card (usually stolen/lost) is altered to have new expiration, account and identification data.

- *White plastic.* In this scheme a business front is opened. Imitations of credit cards with OCR font but no security design are made up usually based upon discarded copy tissues of real cards, and "sales" are recorded. The business front is closed after the credit card company forwards payment for the sales, but before the real card owners can complain about their bills. Alternatively, the scheme can be used by an employee of an existing business.

BIBLIOGRAPHY

Clark, Susan, *et al.* (1995), "Counterfeit Card Fraud," *Royal Canadian Mounted Police (RCMP) Gazette*, 57(10) (October): 2–10.

Levinson, Jay (1982), "The Document Examiner and the Plastic Card," Paper presented at the annual meeting of the American Society of Questioned Document Examiners, Boston, MA.

Morris, Ronald L. *et al.* (1995), "Vacuum Metal Deposition of Silver as an Aid in Credit Card Examinations," *International Journal of Forensic Document Examiners*, 1(4): 272–274.

Sang, John L. and Sang, Hugh L. (1985), "Credit Cards and the Forensic Document Examiner," *Forensic Science International*, 28: 121–129.

Spencer, Rosalind J. (1986), "Multiple-processing of Visa Vouchers," *Journal of the Forensic Science Society*, 26: 401–407.

PROOF OF AGE

In many countries with incomplete or relatively new citizen birth registries it is common that unofficial documents be presented to show age of a person. In many Western countries this usually takes the form of statements of birth inscribed into bibles and prayerbooks. In most cases it is impossible to positively date the writing, particularly if pencil is used. At best, the examiner can usually only make a statement that no evidence could be found to negate the claimed date.

Basing authenticity on the order of entries in a book can be problematic, since this presumes that other entries are genuine and were written at the time of the births indicated.

Negation of a date is more simple and can be based upon earliest manufacture of ink and paper formulae, publication date of a book, etc.

CHECKS

The check is a common method of payment in today's society, and as such it has become a common tool used in fraudulent business transactions. Although there is often talk of the "paperless society," a check still is preferred by many people as an immediate written record of a financial transaction. There are several different types of fraudulent checks:

- *Total forgery.* This type of fraud is relatively rare, since it means investing printing and paper resources to reproduce documents that can be found through other means. The cases involving total forgery tend to be business or bank checks, often made payable for considerable sums of money.
- *Stolen/lost checks.* In these cases the person using the check in question has acquired it as a result of theft/loss. From the document examiner's perspective the first rule is to determine which portions on the face of the check were written by the person passing the check. It is common, for example, for the writer of a check to leave the payee line blank. In certain cases this has been taken to an extreme, and the writer has only signed, dictating date and sum to the check recipient. Sometimes "professional" check-passing rings have different people write different parts of the check to complicate handwriting and possible detection. The entire examination of the check can be voided if it can be shown that the examiner mistook the fill-in of two persons to be the writing of one individual. Quick methods of "one writer" determination are subjective glance and ink differentiation.

    It is common with some document examiners to consider spacing and format (e.g., method of writing the sum) as factors in writer identification. This, of course, should be voided if there is reason to believe that there is a conscious effort to distort natural habits. Another point of frequent distortion is the signature.

    On the face of a check there is usually sufficient handwriting to make a firm conclusion of writer identity. This is important in establishing identity of the actual writer and verifying that the legal check owner was not the writer.
- *Genuine checks from accounts opened in false identities.* This is probably the most common source of fraudulent checks in Israel. From the document examiner's perspective there is little material for a Questioned Documents examination.
- *Altered checks.* Another type of check fraud is to take a genuinely issued check and raise the amount by alteration. This can be done by adding text (such as altering a "1" to "7") or by chemical/physical erasure followed by entering a new text. A basic method to prevent alteration is the use of a check writer (see above).
- *Denied endorsement.* There have been numerous instances, particularly with checks sent

through the mails, where the payee has denied receipt of payment and has stated that he is not responsible for the endorsement. These cases should be handled as regular handwriting/signature cases. Writing in a constricted space, however, should be taken into account.

In earlier days when there were fewer checks in circulation it was common for police departments to maintain a fraudulent check file through which the handwriting on new checks was associated with previous submissions. Today most of these files are being abandoned as being ineffective.

Some police departments treat all checks with ninhydrin to look for fingerprints. When this is done, the checks should be photographed before ninhydrin is used.

As a practical measure in the wake of sheer volume, many police departments have withdrawn from the contention that they must examine all fraudulent checks. The most common criteria today are very large sums and checks related to major crimes. This has most importance for an accused who must consider case consolidation at his trial.

BIBLIOGRAPHY

Altevela, Joseph (1972), *Check Frauds and Forgeries at the Teller's Window*, Financial Publishing Company, Boston, Massachusetts.

Sekharan, P. Chandra (1987), "A Classification System for Identification of Fraudulent Cheques," *Indian Journal of Forensic Sciences*, 1: 53–62.

Sternitzky, Julius (1955), *Forgery and Fictitious Checks*, Charles C. Thomas, Springfield, Illinois.

TRAVELER'S CHECKS

The most common method of forgery connected with traveler's checks is bogus endorsement. Here the forger is relying upon the inability of the recipient to conduct a quick and professional signature examination (technically, not an unfounded supposition!). In most cases a pictorially close signature written without hesitations is sufficient. Recording of passport or driver's license data can provide a recourse to the check passer, but only with the assumption that the documents presented were genuinely issued to that person. (Recording of these items is generally superfluous, since the recipient is guaranteed payment in any case by the check issuing company.)

Figure 16.2

Traveler's check with bogus endorsement. There are numerous differences between the genuine and forged signatures.

Totally counterfeit traveler's checks have been encountered, however the sophisticated security features introduced to many checks in recent years have kept this phenomenon to a minimum.

Another fraud technique is traveler's checks in which the face value has been raised. In several cases of raising, the method encountered was to "sand blast" the old number off by using tiny glass pellets. A new amount was then printed on the check.

One problem encountered with traveler's checks is that unless a problem is caught virtually immediately, the passer is often long gone. With regular checks many recipients require that a local identification be presented. In the case of a traveler's check it is assumed very naturally that the passer is not a local resident.

ANONYMOUS LETTERS

Anonymous letters bother many people. Often the writer will cease writing, usually in annoyance cases where the recipient appears not to react (or at least is not seen or perceived to react). In certain cases, however, particularly in incidents involving criminal acts (most prominently kidnapping cases), it is important to conduct an investigation which includes but is not limited to handwriting. Some police departments have psychologists screen threatening letters to determine which should be taken seriously; this has obvious benefits with the calculated gamble that a serious letter might sometimes be wrongly dismissed.

When these letters are received, they should be handled with care so as not to preclude police examinations such as fingerprints. The letter should also be forwarded for examination with the envelope in which it was received. Tape, stickers, and stamps on the envelope should not be disturbed.

Possible examinations include paper analysis, indented writing (ESDA), watermarks, tears, and envelope sourcing as well as fingerprints and traditional handwriting/typewriting/printing. There have been successes with syntax and vocabulary analysis to direct an investigation, but these methods are of very limited value in courtroom presentation.

BIBLIOGRAPHY

Moreau, Dale M. (n.d.), *Anonymous Letter Cases: The Importance of a Comprehensive Forensic Awareness for the Investigator,"* Federal Bureau of Investigation Academy.

GRAFFITI AND WALL WRITING

For many reasons people have written messages on walls, windows and other such surfaces. These reasons range from a desperate message left by an injured crime victim to messages written with a poor taste of propriety. Examination of this material for writer identification follows the same rules as delineated elsewhere – there must be sufficient writing, and (as strange as it might seem) comparable known writing must be obtained. Due to these limitations, it is rare that an unqualified identification of graffiti authorship is possible through handwriting examination.

Paper can be sent to a laboratory for examination. Although parts of walls can theoretically be removed and shipped, routine cases require extensive photography of the material in question, using different lighting and exposures to record all aspects of the writing.

POSTAGE STAMPS AND CANCELLATIONS

There have been forgeries of both postage stamps and postal cancellations, each for different reasons.

POSTAGE STAMPS

- Valuable stamps. The American Philatelic Society and the American Philatelic Foundation both maintain specific information and expertising services for these stamps.
- Common stamps that are unavailable for some reason. This category most notably includes wartime and intelligence forgeries not available to the combatant (e.g., Western forgeries of German postage during World War I, North Korean forgeries of South Korean postage). Due to the very specialized type of forgeries, cases are quite rare.
- Revenue stamps. Particularly older revenue stamps are sometimes forged to "authenticate" old transactions. This can be done in one of two ways: (1) forgeries are

sometimes printed when unused stamps are not available; (2) alternatively, genuine stamps from other transactions have been lifted and transferred to the bogus paperwork.

Examination should always include verification that the stamps in question were available and valid on the date in question, and that in the case particularly of revenue stamps the sum paid was appropriate. A key source for dates of revenue stamps are specialized stamp catalogs generally available through philatelic stores or associations.

- Meters. There have been cases of falsifying meter impressions to avoid payment of postage. This is rare, except under unusual circumstances, due to the relatively high cost of producing a forgery compared with the price of postage.

- Political forgeries. For numerous reasons there have been stamp forgeries of a political nature. These have ranged from caricatures mocking people on legal postage to forgeries for the simple purpose of mailing letters. These forgeries do not normally find their way into the casework of document examiners and contesting in court. They are more often of interest to stamp collectors and are "authenticated" in philatelic circles. Many forgeries are known from the First and Second World Wars and the aftermath of the Korean confrontation.

BIBLIOGRAPHY – POLITICAL STAMP FORGERIES

Williams, L.N. and Williams, M. (1938), *The "Propaganda" Forgeries: A History and Description of the Austrian, Bavarian and German Stamps Counterfeited by Order of the British Government during the Great War, 1914–1918*, David Field Ltd, London.

CANCELLATIONS

- Valuable cancellations. The American Philatelic Society and the American Philatelic Foundation both maintain specific information and expertising services for these cancellations.

- Dating. There have been numerous instances in which postal cancellations have been forged or altered to establish dating. For example, cases have included dating of a tender response to reflect ostensible mailing before the closing date. These cancellations should be examined similar to cachets. Sometimes it will be necessary to obtain examples of *all* the genuine cancellations in use in the location concerned during the relevant time period. (If cancellations are numbered, for example with the number of the clerk, only cancellations of that number need be compared with the questioned material.) Sometimes cancellations can be shown to be bogus based upon class characteristics (e.g. rubber rather than metal, obsolete format, incorrect order of date information).

BIBLIOGRAPHY – CANCELLATIONS

Perelman, Benjamin (1982), "Case History: Examination of a Postal Cachet," Paper presented at the annual meeting of the American Society of Questioned Document Examiners, Boston, Massachusetts.

LAND TRANSFERS

Modern real estate transactions are generally reflected in formal documents, the validity of which is based upon filing with the appropriate authorities. Ottoman and Mandate Palestine present problems that are typical of many other countries. Land transfers were not often formalized with ruling authorities, and transfer papers that were filed were not always recorded (and when recorded, not necessarily on a timely basis). Also, not all official records are available today. In Europe, for example, many government records regarding land transfers were destroyed during the Second World War.

The authentication of land transfer documentation should be based upon the availability of materials (ink, paper, and revenue stamps) at the time of dating. Use of materials not yet in use on the date of the document is, of course, proof of forgery. Authentication can be difficult to prove, and often the proper conclusion is that "no evidence of forgery was found" or "the document is (appears to be) consistent with documents issued during the period."

Q.   As you know, my client contends that the property in question belongs to him based on a sales receipt dated 1 January 1940. Have you examined the said receipt?

A.   Yes I have.

Q.   Could you please tell us your conclusion.

A.   As I have stated, I have found no evidence of forgery in the questioned receipt.

Q.   Can we then conclude that the document is genuine?

A.   No, I can only say that I found no evidence of forgery.

Q.   Let me re-phrase. Did you find any reason to question the authenticity of the document?

A.   I found no evidence of forgery.

Q.   Please refresh my memory. Which organization certified you as an Examiner of Questioned Documents?

A.   The Forensic Science Society. I have been certified for eight years.

> Q.   And for how long have you been an Examiner of Questioned Documents?
>
> A.   For fifteen years.
>
> Q.   With such credentials it would be hard for me to believe that there could have been signs of forgery which you could not find.

VOTING RECORDS

There are many questions involved in voting records. In Israel, for example, placement on the ballot is contingent upon petition signatures of a certain number of voters. There have been numerous cases in which it was found, through handwriting examination, that one person signed the petition more than once.

There are a number of different methods to list those persons who have already voted on Election Day, so that one person cannot vote twice. In the United States this is generally done by the voter's signing of the voting register. Here, signature forgery is possible. There are two situations which raise particular problems: (1) when a genuine signature is placed in the register in a position where it can be imitated, and (2) where there is no comparison signature available in the register to "authenticate" the voter, who is then called upon to produce identification to authenticate himself. In other countries a mark is made on a national identity card to register the fact that the bearer has voted.

The most common type of voting fraud is casting ballots based upon illegal registration (bogus papers), or voting in the name of people (ill, deceased, away on travel) who cannot cast their own ballots.

DIARIES

The most famous diary forgeries of recent times are probably those supposedly of Benito Mussolini and Adolf Hitler. The forgeries were produced for purely monetary reasons. Other diary forgeries often involve additions or deletions done for personal reasons.

In the case of the Hitler forgery, at first the diary was examined and thought to be authentic. Subsequent handwriting and technical examination showed it to be a forgery.

CAR REGISTRATION AND DRIVERS LICENSES

Car theft is often accompanied by forgery of the registration so that the new owner (at times unwitting, or at least not willing to articulate his suspicions after buying a vehicle at a price way below market value) can use or register the vehicle, or have it inspected for road safety. This forgery can include the basic registration, authenticating seals, and inspection certificates.

Another option for illegally documenting a vehicle is to alter a genuine registration. This can range from changing as little as the license number to altering details describing both vehicle and owner. In most cases every effort will be made not to present bogus papers to official motor vehicle authorities to minimize the chance of detection.

There is generally no problem in gaining genuine copies of official car ownership and registration documents, since these papers are generally standard for defined periods of time, and in most modernized countries they are printed with security features.

BIBLIOGRAPHY

ID Checking Guide, Drivers License Guide Company, Redwood City, California (annual publication appearing in February).

Interpol (1998), *Interpol Guide to Vehicle Registration Documents*, Keesing Reference Systems, Amsterdam, Netherlands (coverage of Europe and neighboring countries only).

BIRTH CERTIFICATES

In many countries it is extremely difficult to authenticate birth certificates. In the United States, for example, there are over 7000 jurisdictions with the authority to issue birth certificates, yet together with this authority there are no standards, forms change without notice, and authenticating signatures. In the United States it is, perhaps, relatively simple albeit time-consuming to have the issuing office certify its earlier paperwork.

This is much more complicated in other countries in which war and other circumstances destroyed government records. To cite the example of Poland, the wide variety of pre-Second World War birth certificates and the inability to authenticate them allowed Resistance forces to obtain genuine identity cards based upon forged birth papers.

In Israel the problem of immigrants' certificates remains, however Israeli birth records are now computerized with certificates based upon national standards.

The document examiner has the practical problem that without certified known certificates from the questioned period of issuance, it is not possible to conduct a meaningful examination.

BIBLIOGRAPHY

Kusserow, Richard P. (1988), *Birth Certificate Fraud*, US Government Printing Office, Washington, DC.

APPENDIX I

COURTROOM TESTIMONY – SAMPLE QUESTIONS

QUALIFYING THE WITNESS

Q.   Please state your name.

A.   Dr Jay Levinson.

Q.   Since when were you a document examiner?

A.   1972.

Q.   Could you please tell the court, who supervised your training as a document examiner?

A.   Dr David Crown.

Q.   Please tells us something about this person's professional background.

A.   Dr Crown began his career with the United States Post Office Documents Laboratory in 1957. In 1968 he transferred to the United States Central Intelligence Agency where he was head of the Documents Laboratory. He has also served as president of both the American Academy of Forensic Sciences and the American Society of Questioned Document Examiners.

Q.   Please describe your professional training under his supervision.

A.   I started my training in 1972. I was assigned a reading program that covered a wide range of literature in the field as well as supervised casework.

Q.   Did you receive any other training?

A.   Yes. I did supervised casework. In addition I took a course in typewriter examination at Georgetown University from Mr Ordway Hilton.

Q.   How long was your training?

A.   I was considered a trainee for three years, however even after that initial period I have made continuous efforts to sharpen my skills and update myself on new developments in the field.

Q.   Are you a member of any professional organizations?

A.   Yes. I passed the entrance tests, and I was accepted as a regular member of the American Society of Questioned Documents Examiners. My professional credentials were also certified by the American Board of Forensic Document Examiners, and I was elected to diplomate status.

DISQUALIFYING THE WITNESS

Q.   Are you a member of any professional organization?

A.   Yes, I am a member of the International X Society.

Q.   Can you tell me what qualifies you to be a member?

A.   Yes, I have paid an initiation fee and I have paid dues for the past five years.

Q.   Are there any other requirements to be a member?

A.   No.

Q.   Have you ever passed a proficiency test?

A.   No.

Q.   Have you ever been certified as a document examiner?

A.   No.

Q.   Have you ever worked under a trained examiner?

A.   No.

Q.   Who did train you?

A.   I took a correspondence course from the American Correspondence School.

Q.   Perhaps you can tell us a little about this school.

A.   Yes, they offer courses in some one hundred disciplines.

Q.   All related to documents?

A   No. These courses range from mechanics to weather forecasting.

Q.   Is document examination your main profession?

A   No. I am a full-time teacher of geography.

Q.   How many document cases did you examine last year?

A   Three or four.

Q.   And do you feel that is sufficient to maintain your skills?
A.   Yes.

Q.   Have you ever published an article?
A.   No.

Q.   Have you ever presented a paper at a conference?
A.   No.

GRAPHOLOGY

Q.   According to your written expert testimony you are a graphologist.
A.   That is correct. I have been a graphologist for the past sixteen years.

Q.   Could you please tell us what is graphology?
A.   Yes. It is the determination of personality traits through handwriting.

Q.   I assume that you do this commercially. Is that so?
A.   Yes. I do receive a fee for my opinions.

Q.   Could you please tell the court who seeks your services?
A.   My primary clients are companies seeking advice on hiring new employees. They send applications to me. I also advise on marriage issues.

Q.   This does not really sound relevant to determining if the same writer prepared two different documents. Do you handle this type of case as well?
A.   Yes, I do. I made three or four examinations of this sort in the past year.

Q.   Did you receive training for this type of examination?
A.   Yes, I did. It is clear that if two specimens of writing show different character traits, it is not possible that they were written by the same person.

INTRODUCING EVIDENCE

Q.   Could you please tell the court which documents you examined in this case?
A.   Six checks were submitted for examination. As is noted in my case file, I received them on 1 June of this year. I labeled the checks Q 1–6 and initialed each in the lower right corner of the front side.

Q.   Which examination was requested?

A.   I was requested to determine if these checks were filled out and signed by the defendant, Mr John Smith.

Q.   Please explain to the Court how you proceeded in your examination.

A.   I requested "course of business" writing of a similar nature and of the same time period from Mr Smith. In this case I received twenty canceled checks from his account, No. 135246 in Hometown Bank, Downtown Branch. The checks were written within six weeks of the Questioned checks. Again, I labeled these checks K 1–20 and initialed each in the lower right hand corner.

Q.   Is that all?

A.   No. I also asked that Mr Smith come to our laboratory to write dictated specimens. Mr Smith signed a statement, labeled K-0 and appropriately initialed, that he was giving this writing of his own free will. I then dictated the text of ten checks and asked that he write the information on forms similar to checks; these are initialed and labeled K 21–30. Each check was removed from sight before the next dictation began.

Q.   Would it not have been easier to have Mr Smith copy a written text?

A.   Yes, it might have been easier. I did not do that to insure that Mr Smith would not be influenced by spelling, layout, or any other feature of such a text.

EXAMINER'S CASE FILE

Q.   Can you please tell us how you conducted your examination?

A.   First I examined the Questioned material to verify that it was filled out in normal writing. I then examined each Questioned check separately. I listed the basic individualities in the sum line (words and digits), then I made a separate list of individualities in the signature. Finally, I compared all of my notes so that I could have an overall picture of the writer's range of variation. This is also a check that there are no unexplained inconsistencies in any of the writings.

Q.   You have not mentioned the "payee" line. Why is that?

A.   On most of the Questioned checks I found that the payee line was written in an ink different from the rest of the check. This is highly suggestive of another writer. In my examination I, therefore, discounted all of the payee line writing.

Q.   Is everything written in your case file?
A.   I recorded all of my examinations in the case file. My notes are also in the file.

Q.   Then . . .
A.   Next, I went through similar procedures with K 1–20 (course of business writing) and K 21–30 (specimens which I dictated to the defendant). At the end of this process I had a good idea of the range of variation and writing individualities in the known writing. Finally, I compared the Questioned and Known and came to my conclusion.

WORDING OF THE CONCLUSION

Q.   Can you please tell the Court what your conclusion was.
A.   With your permission, please allow me to read from my Statement of Expert Opinion:

It is my professional opinion that Q 1–6 (amounts and signature) were written by the writer of K 1–30.

Q.   That is to say that the writing was done by the defendant, Mr Smith?
A.   Yes.

Q.   Is it possible that someone else wrote the Questioned writings?
A.   We can have philosophical discussions that "anything is possible," but in real terms I have absolutely no doubt. The defendant wrote the Questioned writing, and no one else.

ALTERNATIVE CONCLUSION

Q.   Can you please tell the Court what your conclusion was.
A.   With your permission, please allow me to read from my Statement of Expert Opinion:

It is my professional opinion that Q 1–6 (amounts and signature) were probably written by the writer of K 1–30.

Q.   Could you explain what do you mean by "probably?"
A   Yes. I cannot absolutely rule out another writer.

Q.   Does that mean there is a 60% chance that "K" wrote the Questioned material?

A.   I really do not want to express myself in numerical terms. My intention is that I cannot totally exclude another writer, however there certainly are not many writers who could have written the material. If I had significant doubts, I would have said, "K as well as other writers *could have written* the Questioned material."

QUALITY ASSURANCE – CASTING DOUBT

Q.   Does your laboratory have certification?

A.   No, but we are supervised by the Provincial Ministry of Justice.

Q.   Does the Ministry have set written standards for how the laboratory is to function?

A.   No, not really.

Q.   Do you have all the professional literature available in your library?

A.   Yes, we do have a library.

Q.   No, that is not what I asked you. Do you have all of the significant books on Questioned Documents?

Q.   Does that library receive journals so that you have access to the latest professional literature?

Q.   Do you have all of the equipment available to do a complete examination?

Q.   Do you have written rules to guide you on examination procedures?

Q.   When is the last time you completed a proficiency test?

Q.   Let me summarize, if I might. Am I to understand that no outside group checks your work.
     You decide what books are important enough to buy. You decide before reading a book that it is not worth buying.
     You decide that you have enough equipment to do every examination needed.
     You have no written work rules, so no one can really decide if you have worked properly.

In the past year you have not had a proficiency test – in other words a test with a known answer.

Despite this you are testifying with the contention that the conclusion in your examination is correct. How can we really be certain?

Q.   Just one final question. Part of Quality Assurance is compliance with ISO requirements and recommendations. Could you please explain what these are, and how your laboratory complies?

APPENDIX II

LATIN CHARACTER TYPEFONT
IDENTIFICATION SYSTEMS

DURANTAYE

Coverage
Modern Latin alphabet typefonts in use in Canada.

Source
de la Durantaye, Gerard A. (1968, rev. 1973), "Revised Classification of Type-styles (1973)," Centre of Forensic Sciences, Toronto. Unpublished. Also, "A Classification System for Typewriting Specimens," *Canadian Society of Forensic Science Journal*, 1: 61–64.

Description
The examiner is required to determine basic style (monotone, cubic, etc.) of the typefont in question. In monotone, for example, he must then measure the pitch, then he has to describe the letters t / f / g / M / 3 / 4 (and sometimes W) according to multiple choice questions.

Benefits
A certain amount of dating material is included in the scheme.

Disadvantages
Although some European typewriters are included, the database is decidedly North American.

CROWN

Coverage
1968 – elite and pica monotone fonts of non-USA manufacture. Latin alphabet.
1976 – Pica monotone fonts of US and foreign manufacture. Latin alphabet.

Source
Crown, David A. (1968), "Class Characteristics of Foreign Typewriters and

Typefaces," *Journal of Criminal Law, Criminology and Police Science,* 59(2): 298–323.
Crown, David A. (1976), "Differentiation of Pica Monotone Typewriting," *Journal of Police Science and Administration,* 4(3): 134–178.

Description

In 1968 Crown published a differentiation scheme covering some 150 elite and pica monotone typefonts of non-US manufacture. According to the system, the examiner must look at a series of letters and determine their category according to definitions given by Crown. After the examiner has made a sufficient number of differentiation decisions, he will be able to conclude which typefont was used to prepare the document in question. Next, the examiner turns to a table arranged according to pitch, where he can find out on which typewriters and in which years specific typefonts were used. Finally, a supplement to the 1968 article lists information about typewriter manufacturing companies. In 1976, Crown issued an updated scheme covering only pica monotone, but including typefonts of US manufacture.

Benefits of the scheme

This is a comprehensive scheme for the subject, and every effort was made to include as many monotone fonts as possible, including many that are quite rare.

Drawbacks

1. The system is cumbersome to use, and the examiner would best receive training and exercise in its operation.
2. The lack of accompanying specimens precludes the examiner from checking his work.
3. Since the examiner must progress in the scheme from one letter decision to another, he is faced with a problem if key letters are missing. (This is particularly common when examining a text in a Romance language, where "w," the second letter in the scheme, is rarely found.)
4. Many of the letter distinctions are hard to see and rather subjective.

HAAS

Coverage

Latin fonts.

Sources

Haas, Josef (1959), "Determining the Make and Model of Typewriters Based on Elite Type," *Archiv fuer Kriminologie,* 123(3–4): 65–87.
Haas, Josef (1972), *Atlas der Schreibmaschinenschrift Pica,* Private Publication, West Germany.

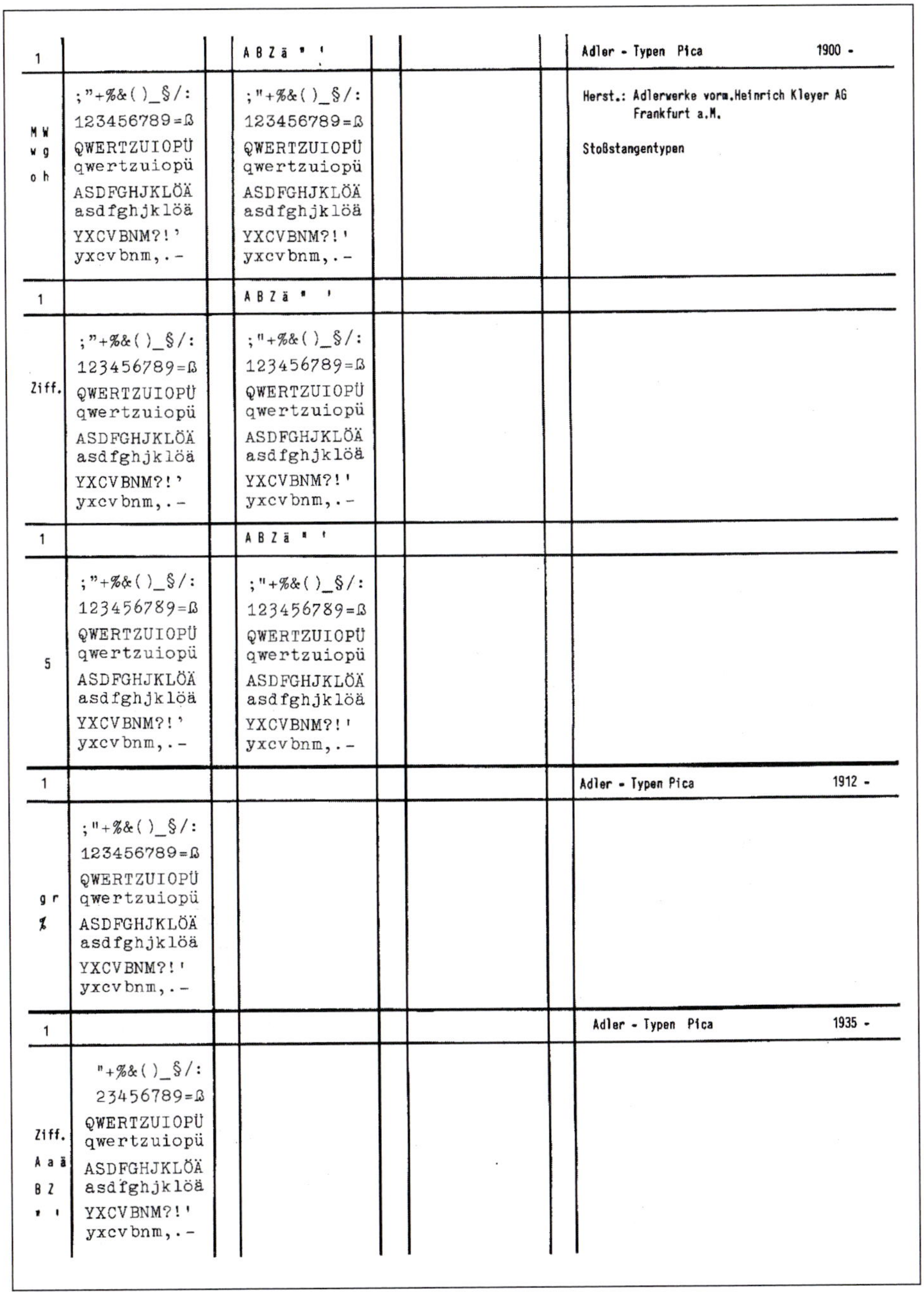
1 | | A B Z ä " ' | | Adler - Typen Pica 1900 -

M W w g o h | ;"+%&()_§/: 123456789=ß QWERTZUIOPÜ qwertzuiopü ASDFGHJKLÖÄ asdfghjklöä YXCVBNM?!' yxcvbnm,.- | ;"+%&()_§/: 123456789=ß QWERTZUIOPÜ qwertzuiopü ASDFGHJKLÖÄ asdfghjklöä YXCVBNM?!' yxcvbnm,.- | | Herst.: Adlerwerke vorm.Heinrich Kleyer AG Frankfurt a.M. Stoßstangentypen

1 | | A B Z ä " '

Ziff. | ;"+%&()_§/: 123456789=ß QWERTZUIOPÜ qwertzuiopü ASDFGHJKLÖÄ asdfghjklöä YXCVBNM?!' yxcvbnm,.- | ;"+%&()_§/: 123456789=ß QWERTZUIOPÜ qwertzuiopü ASDFGHJKLÖÄ asdfghjklöä YXCVBNM?!' yxcvbnm,.-

1 | | A B Z ä " '

5 | ;"+%&()_§/: 123456789=ß QWERTZUIOPÜ qwertzuiopü ASDFGHJKLÖÄ asdfghjklöä YXCVBNM?!' yxcvbnm,.- | ;"+%&()_§/: 123456789=ß QWERTZUIOPÜ qwertzuiopü ASDFGHJKLÖÄ asdfghjklöä YXCVBNM?!' yxcvbnm,.-

1 | | | | Adler - Typen Pica 1912 -

g r % | ;"+%&()_§/: 123456789=ß QWERTZUIOPÜ qwertzuiopü ASDFGHJKLÖÄ asdfghjklöä YXCVBNM?!' yxcvbnm,.-

1 | | | | Adler - Typen Pica 1935 -

Ziff. A a ä B Z " ' | "+%&()_§/: 23456789=ß QWERTZUIOPÜ qwertzuiopü ASDFGHJKLÖÄ asdfghjklöä YXCVBNM?!' yxcvbnm,.-

Figure A.1

Example of specimens from the 1972 Haas Atlas. Note the totally regular quality of the "specimens" and the German keyboard arrangement.

Figure A.1
(Continued)

GRUNDFORMEN PICA

Beschaffenheit und Länge der Mittelstriche

1. mit Ansatz   2. ohne Ansatz   3. ohne Ansatz
   hoch   hoch   tief

(gleiche Formen auch bei der Majuskel "W")

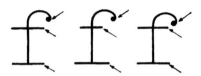

Länge der Horizontalstriche, Lage des Kopfpunktes

1. gleich lang   2. ungleich lang   3. gleich lang
   Kp hoch   Kp hoch/tief   Kp tief

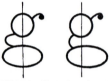

Mittelsenkrechte des Kreiselementes
teilt das Ovalelement in

1. etwa gleich   2. deutlich ungleich
   große Hälften   große Hälften

Schlußhäkchen

1. vorhanden   2. nicht vorhanden

(Achtung auf Typendefekt! Kontrolle bei Umlaut ä)

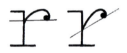

Ansatz und Kopfpunkt des Bogens
befinden sich

1. etwa auf   2. deutlich auf
   gleicher Höhe   ungleicher Höhe

Verlängerung des unteren Schrägstriches
verläuft vom Scheitelpunkt des Horizontalstriches

1. links   2. rechts

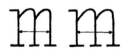

Breite des Schriftzeichens
(von Strichmitte zur Strichmitte)
1. bis 1,70 mm   2. ab 1,75 mm

Breite des Bogens
(von Strichmitte zur Strichmitte)
1. bis 1,00 mm   2. ab 1,05 mm

Länge des Basisstriches
(von Winkelmitte zur Ansatzmitte)
1. bis 1,70 mm   2. ab 1,75 mm

Haas, Josef und Haas, Bernhard (1985–1986 and updates), *Atlas der Schreib-maschinenschriften*, Private Publication, West Germany.

Also see: Bouffard, Philip D. (1988), "An Index to Typestyles in the Haas Non-Pica Atlas," paper presented at the annual meeting of the American Society of Questioned Document Examiners, Denver, Colorado.

Description

These three publications give quite complete coverage of Latin key/bar fonts. In the 1972 edition there are cards with holes to help the examiner sort characteristics of letters and to arrive at the font sought. (Remember that this was in the pre-personal computer age!) In both the 1972 and 1985/6 books notation is made of the differences between various fonts. The 1972 volume is based upon drawings of the fonts; the later Atlas has actual strike-ups (impressions made from typewriters).

Benefits

The Haas collection provides a reasonably complete collection of fonts and their usage on typewriters (particularly for the German market).

Drawbacks

1. The 1972 cards are effective only for German language letter frequency.
2. Many of the differences are "real," but they are so minute that they cannot be detected in a typewritten document.
3. The 1972 Atlas (one volume) and the 1985/6 Atlas (two volumes) are extremely expensive.

INTERPOL

Coverage

Latin alphabet type fonts of various styles with emphasis on French keyboard specimens.

Source

Interpol (1969), *System for Identification of Typewriter Makes Using the Card Index*, ICPO – Interpol General Secretariat, January 1969 (with periodic updates of the specimen cards, now discontinued).

Description

Two identical cards of each typewriter specimen are supplied to the user.

The first card, labeled in capital letters with the name of the typewriter manufacturer, is filed alphabetically. This file is used when an examiner is looking for a specimen prepared on the typewriter of a specific manufacturer.

The second card is filed according to an identification formula as follows:

$$\text{letter spacing} / t / \text{digits} / f / M$$

Letter spacing is defined as the number of mm/character. "t" and "f" are questions if the horizontal crossbar is symmetrical or asymmetrical. The examiner is also requested to determine if the digits are closed-looped or open-squared. A typical differentiation formula would be:

$$220 / 2 / a / 2 / A$$

Once the examiner has determined the formula in the document that he is examining, he then locates that group of cards in the file with the same formula. He then selects those cards with the same font as the document in question. (It should be stressed that there is often more than one card with the same typefont. The principle reason is that the Interpol system is based upon typewriters rather than typefont. Thus, a new card is made for each typewriter even though the font already appears in the file.)

Each card contains further information about the typewriter and the font.

The Interpol system was initiated in 1969. It was discontinued in the mid-1980s.

Drawbacks

1. The system is based upon typewriters, and even when typefont information is provided, it is often only fragmentary.
2. An inexperienced examiner might make the mistake of thinking that the collection contains all usage of a particular font.
3. Updates to the collection were incomplete in the few years previous to discontinuing the system.

Benefits

1. The system contains some two thousand (2000) typewriter specimens according to a standard formula.
2. The specimens allow you to check your results.
3. The specimens from French keyboard typewriters are particularly strong.

```
CONSUL (C.S.)                Formule  250 | 2 | b | 2 | A

Modéle : 221 Manuelle
Fabricant : CONSUL (CS)              Hauteur du "M" : 2,60 mm
Lieu de fabrication : BRNO (CS)      Hauteur du "u" : 2,05 mm
Année : 1971                         Motion : 6,7 mm
Matricule : 1.221.107356             Largeur max papier : 255 mm
Typé de caractéres : PICA P1         Type de clavier : Français
Fabrique de caractéres : ZETA (CS)   Interlignes : 4,25 & 6,37 mm


    C L A V I E R    11  22  33  44  55  66  77  88  99  &&  °°  mm³
                     ½½  éé  ""  ''  ((  —   èè  __  çç  àà  ))  mm²

                     AA  ZZ  EE  RR  TT  YY  UU  II  OO  PP  ¨¨
                     aa  zz  ee  rr  tt  yy  uu  ii  oo  pp  ^^

                     QQ  SS  DD  FF  GG  HH  JJ  KK  LL  MM  %%
                     qq  ss  dd  ff  gg  hh  jj  kk  ll  mm  ùù

                     WW  XX  CC  VV  BB  NN  ??  ..  //  ++
                     ww  xx  cc  vv  bb  nn  ,,  ;;  ::  ==


  1°interligne : peux-tu m'envoyer de ce bon vieux whisky, comme celui que
                 j'ai bu chez françois le frére du forgeron du village.
  2°interligne : PEUX-TU M'ENVOYER DE CE BONVVIEUX WHISKY, COMME CELUI QUE
                 J4AI BU CHEZ FRANCOIS LE FRERE DU FORGERON DU VILLAGE.


              26.09.72                        Fiche n° 999
```

Figure A.2

Sample Interpol specimen card. One of the problems with the Interpol system is that the difference between IBM (USA) and IBM World Trade Company (Europe) is not as clear as it should be.

HILTON

Coverage

American-made pica monotone fonts manufactured 1920–1954.

Source

Hilton, Ordway (1956), *Scientific Examination of Documents*, Callaghan & Company, Chicago, Illinois, pp. 48–55.

Note: The scheme is based upon the article, Hilton, Ordway (1951), "A Systematic Method for Identifying the Make and Age-Model of a Typewriter from Its Work," *American Journal of Police Science*, 41(5): 661–674. This article also mentions elite.

Description

In total the system covers 35 typefonts and allows the examiner to draw conclusions about letter design, decide upon a font manufacturer/style (in the traditional American practice the font manufacturer is usually the typewriter manufacturer), then check his work against a specimen. It should be taken into account that when the scheme was published in 1956, it was designed for the situation in America. At that time, foreign manufacturer fonts and typewriters were relatively rare.

Drawbacks
Today this scheme is used for specialized problems.

Benefits
Although the scheme covers only very limited material, the coverage is in depth.

BLACK

Coverage
Selected IBM fonts as of 1968.

Source
Black, David A. (1968), "Differentiating IBM Special Typefonts from Close-Copies," Paper presented at the annual meeting of the American Society of Questioned Document Examiners, 1968.

Description
Several IBM fonts are listed. Their basic features are described, and differences with imitations are listed.

Benefits
The information is concise, and the author has appended all required specimens so that the examiner can check his conclusions.

Drawbacks
The material is dated. A large number of imitation fonts was released to the market after 1968, including many copies of IBM which can be extremely difficult to discern.

DIXON

Coverage
Imitations of key IBM (USA) fonts.

Source
Dixon, Kent C. (1976), "Most Easily Recognized Characteristics Differentiating

IBM Special Typefonts from Copies," Paper presented at American Academy of Forensic Science Annual Meeting, Washington, DC.

Description
Specific comparisons between IBM fonts and "close-similars" are made, highlighting differences.

Benefits
The material is clear, and the enlarged drawings of the fonts make differentiation points stand out.

Drawbacks
The scheme is limited to IBM, SCM (Smith Corona), Remington, Underwood, and Royal. No actual specimens are included.

CROMWELL

Coverage
Pica "Courier" fonts in the Latin alphabet.

Source
Cromwell, Douglas (1973), "A Method of Indicating the Manufacture of Courier Style Type Fonts," *Journal of Police Science and Administration*, 1(3): 303–310.

Description
After a basic definition of "Courier" is given, twelve specimens of these fonts are given in three separate charts (lower case, upper case, digits and symbols). Then, a differentiation scheme allows identification of the fonts based upon the letters, "b," "c," "k," "l," "o," "r," "s." Other differences between fonts are also given, along with dates of manufacture.

Drawbacks
The scheme represents a very early stage in the development of Courier font, before it was adopted as a popular industry standard. Hence, in today's terms the scheme is very incomplete.

Benefits
The scheme contains a wealth of dating information.

BOUFFARD

Source

Bouffard, Philip D. (1993), "A PC Based Typewriter Classification System for Prestige Typestyle Specimens from the Haas Typewriter Atlas," Paper presented at the annual meeting of the American Society of Questioned Document Examiners, Ottawa, Ontario.

Description

Verbal description and computer program to retrieve information in the Haas collection.

APPENDIX III
ARABIC CHARACTER TYPEFONTS

LEVINSON

Source

Levinson, Jay (1974), "Differentiation of Arabic Type Fonts," Paper presented at the annual meeting of the American Society of Questioned Document Examiners, Milwaukee, Wisconsin.

Supplemented by unpublished font collection, Israel Police, Jerusalem, 1983.

Description

Concentration on Arabic, not Persian. Descriptive material about fonts is given with a differentiation scheme and chart of usage.

Drawbacks

Coverage is only partial.

APPENDIX IV

HEBREW CHARACTER TYPEFONTS

LEVINSON

Source

Levinson, Jay (1983, 1998), "Collection of Hebrew Typefonts," unpublished research paper, Israel Police, Jerusalem.

Description

Copies of Hebrew typewriter fonts and their usage. Some coverage of Yiddish. A chart is included showing the pitch in which fonts were known to have been used.

Drawbacks

Many of the older fonts are represented in only partial strike-ups of poor quality. There is no full differentiation scheme.

APPENDIX V
QUESTIONED DOCUMENT ORGANIZATIONS

AMERICAN ACADEMY OF FORENSIC SCIENCES

Document section. Election as provisional member, member or fellow. Condition of past provisional member attendance at minimum of two annual meetings. Corresponding member category discontinued. No examination required for membership.

Publication of the Academy: *Journal of Forensic Sciences* (bi-monthly).

AMERICAN BOARD OF FORENSIC DOCUMENT EXAMINERS

Certifying board for document examiners resident in the United States and Canada. Certification is by examination with requirements of further education for continuing qualification.

AMERICAN BOARD OF FORENSIC EXAMINERS
AMERICAN BOARD OF FORENSIC HANDWRITING ANALYSTS

As of 1993 renamed American Board of Forensic Examiners. Originally restricted to handwriting and behavioral examinations. Now includes other forensic fields. Certification offered.

AMERICAN SOCIETY OF QUESTIONED DOCUMENT EXAMINERS

Regular membership by examination. Other forms of membership by peer recommendation. Annual meeting with workshops and presentation of professional papers. Publications: Index of ASQDE Papers. (Various volumes covering the period since 1930), journal initiated in 1998 and scheduled to be twice yearly.

http://www.asqde.org

ASSOCIATION OF FORENSIC DOCUMENT EXAMINERS

Founded in 1986. Annual meeting with instructional sessions and professional papers. The Association has its own certification program.

Publication: *Journal of Forensic Document Examination.* Est. 1987.

AUSTRALIAN AND NEW ZEALAND FORENSIC SCIENCE SOCIETY

Established in 1971. The Society encompasses the broad spectrum of Forensic Science including Questioned Documents. Regional meetings and an annual general meeting are held. Membership is open to residents of Australia and New Zealand without examination.

BRITISH ACADEMY OF FORENSIC SCIENCES

Includes Documents section. No examination for entrance.

Publication: *Medicine, Science and the Law* (quarterly).

CANADIAN FORENSIC SCIENCE SOCIETY

Documents section. Acceptance based upon recommendation without examination.

Society publication: *Journal of the Canadian Society of Forensic Science* (quarterly).

DOCUMENT EXAMINERS OF THE WASHINGTON AREA

An informal group of area document examiners who meet at a quarterly luncheon for a program often with guest speaker. There is no formal membership in the group.

EUROPEAN NETWORK OF FORENSIC HANDWRITING EXPERTS (ENFHEX)

Publishes *ENFHEX News* that was started in December 1997. First meeting 17–18 June 1997 based upon a decision taken at the Fifth Conference for Police and Government Handwriting Experts in November 1996. Open to employees of European police and government laboratories and to invitees.

Publication: *ENFHEX News.*

FORENSIC SCIENCE SOCIETY

Stuart Kind started the FSS as the Society for Forensic Science in 1958. The first formal meeting was held at the University of Nottingham on 31 October 1959, and the organization name was changed to the Forensic Science Society. At least two symposia per year are held on forensic science topics including Questioned Documents.

Document section. Membership by recommendation without examination.

Publication: *Science and Justice*, formerly *Journal of the Forensic Science Society* (quarterly).

FORENSIC SCIENCE SOCIETY OF INDIA

Includes Questioned Documents section. Membership by dues payment without professional examination. Recently dormant.

Publication: *Journal of the Forensic Science Society of India* (quarterly).

INDEPENDENT ASSOCIATION OF QUESTIONED DOCUMENT EXAMINERS

Document examiners organization that offers programs for training and certification. Includes graphology.

Publication: *Insight*.

INDO-PACIFIC ASSOCIATION ON LEGAL MEDICINE AND SCIENCE (INPALMS)

General Forensic Science organization covering the Pacific Rim and Asia, with a triennial meeting. Questioned Documents section. Past congresses: Singapore (1983), Colombo (1986), Madras (1989), Bangkok (1992), Bali (1995), Kobe (1998). Meeting scheduled for Melbourne (2001). Abstracts book usually published. No formal membership requirements.

INTERNATIONAL ASSOCIATION FOR IDENTIFICATION

General organization with emphasis on fingerprints and voice identification. Document section.

Publication: Currently, *Journal of Forensic Identification*. Formerly called *Identification News*.

INTERNATIONAL ASSOCIATION OF FORENSIC SCIENCES

This is a general forensic science organization run by a council of past presidents who choose a new member every three years with the goal that said person run a conference three years hence. Questioned Documents is one of the disciplines included in each conference. These meetings have been held in Bruxelles/Ghent (1957), New York (1960), London (1963), Copenhagen (1966), Toronto (1969), Edinburgh (1972), Zurich (1975), Wichita (1979), Bergen (1981), Oxford (1984), Vancouver (1987), Adelaide (1990), Dusseldorf (1993), Tokyo (1996), Los Angeles (1999). The next meeting is due to be held in Montpelier, France (2002). It is IAFS custom to issue a book of abstracts with the conference. ASQDE has held its annual meeting in conjunction with IAFS.

NATIONAL ASSOCIATION OF DOCUMENT EXAMINERS

Established in 1980. Membership by payment of dues. Open to persons in all aspects of document examination including auxiliary fields such as security personnel and law enforcement officers. The newsletter, *Communique*, is published bi-monthly. The *NADE Journal* is published quarterly. The *NADE Journal Digest* is published as a periodic reference guide.

WORLD ASSOCIATION OF QUESTIONED DOCUMENT EXAMINERS

Offers certification. Membership by paying initiation fee and annual dues; testing for membership not required.

Note: Several regional forensic science groups in the United States include members who are document examiners; others are for document examiners only. Informal membership with no testing required before joining. These include:

Mid-Atlantic Association of Forensic Scientists (MAAFS)
Midwestern Association of Forensic Scientists (MAFS)
New Jersey Association of Forensic Scientists
North-eastern Association of Forensic Scientists (NEAFS)
Northwest Association of Forensic Scientists (NWAF)
Southeastern Association of Forensic Document Examiners (SAFDE)
Southern Association of Forensic Scientists (SAFS)
Southwestern Association of Forensic Scientists (SWAFS)

APPENDIX VI

PUBLICATIONS

In addition to journals published by the various societies and associations listed above, there are a number of general forensic science and private publications which publish articles on Questioned Documents:

Archiv fuer Kriminologie (German)
Forensic Science International
Hefte fuer Schriftvergleichen (German)
International Criminal Police Review (Interpol – in English, French, Spanish, Arabic)
International Journal of Forensic Document Examiners (last issue 2000)
Kriminalistik (in German)

INDEX